Le Corbusier's Firminy Church

Introduction by Anthony Eardley

Published by the Institute for Architecture and Urban Studies and Rizzoli International Publications, Inc.

Catalogue 14
April 29 to June 3, 1981

Contents

First published in the United States of America in 1981 by Rizzoli International Publications, Inc. 712 Fifth Avenue, New York, N.Y. 10019

Library of Congress Catalogue Card Number 80-54702
ISBN 0-8478-0380-5

Typography by Myrel Chernick
Printed by Morgan Press, Inc.

Acknowledgments

Peter Eisenman

Le Corbusier's Firminy Church, an exhibition mounted by the Institute for Architecture and Urban Studies and the Cooper Union School of Architecture in the Spring of 1981, owes its inception to the College of Architecture, University of Kentucky, Lexington, with the assistance of Dr. Lewis W. Cochran, Vice President for Academic Affairs.

However, without the ceaseless energy and committment of José Oubrerie, formerly of the Atelier Le Corbusier, both in curating and mounting the exhibition the project would have never been brought to a successful conclusion.

We would also like to thank William Lacy and Leo Kaplan, President and Provost of the Cooper Union for the Advancement of Science and Art, for their sponsorship of this exhibition. We are also indebted to Professor Robert Slutzky, of the School of Architecture at the Cooper Union, for his active assistance in staging the Cooper Union Section of the exhibition.

We are grateful to Daniel Cameron, Exhibition Coordinator at the Institute and to Lindsay Stamm who acted as a curatorial consultant. Kirkor Kalayciyan also played an essential role in realizing the exhibition in his capacity as assistant to José Oubrerie. Sam Flax, Inc. was generous enough to contribute printing services, and the Cooper Union Design Center donated its graphic expertise.

Particular acknowledgment should also be given to Anthony Eardley, Dean of the College of Architecture at the University of Kentucky, whose critical essay included in this publication is both a precise account of the development of the project and a rigorous analysis of its relation to several other religious and secular institutions projected and realized by Le Corbusier.

Finally homage has to be paid to Eugène Claudius-Petit without whose enthusiastic support Le Corbusier's postwar career would not have prospered and the Firminy Church would not have been commissioned. He continues to be owed untold gratitude for his present tireless efforts to raise the funds to complete the church.

1

Atelier Le Corbusier, 35 Rue de Sèvres, 1964.

1 House of Culture and of Youth, Firminy, 1960-1965. Le Corbusier. West facade.

2 Unité D'Habitation, *Firminy, 1963-1968. Le Corbusier. Detail of facade.*

3 Eugène Claudius-Petit and Le Corbusier.

1

2

3

Le Corbusier at Firminy

Eugène Claudius-Petit

We met in the fall of 1944, and in January 1946, Le Corbusier and I sailed on the liberty ship Vernon S. Hood to New York. Over the course of the passage, Le Corbusier finished working out the Modulor, which he showed to his friends with childlike pleasure (as well as later to Albert Einstein in Princeton, who fully appreciated this "language of proportions"). The seventeen days of the voyage allowed us to get to know each other. I had read some of his writing; now I saw the man in the light of his daily life and listened to him endlessly as our friendship became established.

We were in the United States on a mission to meet some architects and also to study the development of the built domain of America. Our first visit was to Lilienthal, the director of the Tennessee Valley Authority in Knoxville. Our major concern was the organization of the land. Everything depended on it: communication, transportation, urbanism, housing, technology, individual life. But my discovery of America with Le Corbusier was also the discovery of this man, whose talent was as yet untapped, whose sensibility was so acute that he could not only discover in the movement of people in the city problems to combat but also imagine their possible solutions.

Given this experience, it was quite natural that I should have a hand in the birth of the *Unité* of Marseilles and have the subsequent pleasure of assuring its completion. It was equally natural for me to encourage the special envoy of President Nehru to entrust the plan for Chandigarh and the construction of the Capitol to Le Corbusier. His nomination as the French expert for the United Nations Complex and as principal consultant for the UNESCO building was also in the order of things. And it was just as much in this general order that I should ask him to work on Firminy as soon as I became mayor, and that he should accept.

Marseilles has its Radiant City. Arbresle has its convent, Ronchamp its chapel, Saint-Dié its factories for the modern epoch, Poissy its Villa Savoye. But in Firminy Le Corbusier built the House of Culture and of Youth, the Olympic stadium, a *Unité d'Habitation,* and his last work, the church of Firminy-Vert, which is still under construction. Thus, after Chandigarh, Firminy is the place that contains the greatest number of buildings by this architect. But why? As mayor of that town from 1953 to 1971, I simply asked him to work as any other mayor of a large town could have done—and he was happy to do so in a town made up of metalworkers and miners. And then, friendship held us together.

It should be emphasized that his realizations in Firminy were not expensive. The House of Culture was built for the same price per square meter as a *Habitation à Loyer Modéré.* But the presence of Architecture is unmistakable, and people come from around the world to see it. The *Unité* is a H.L.M. built within the narrow constraints of the budget, and the church was conceived of in the same manner. The magnificence is in the space, the proportions, the volume, the form.

But this church has known many difficulties, indeed all difficulties imaginable. Yet if faith in a work is attested to by faith itself, we must today continue to hope as he did. "A job was entrusted to me, I did it conscientiously... I struggled with materials, forms, and the trades. I carried out all the conditions of the contract. I did my work, and I feel more bound than ever to this talk of ours...I cannot conceive of anything else at this point than the beginning of construction, for the great joy of all," wrote Le Corbusier to the Abbé Tardy, pastor of Firminy-Vert, on January 28, 1965. Construction began. Then it came to a stop. It started anew. The construction company went under. But everything is starting up again, and the help of many people is awaited.

Sometimes one lets oneself dream. Whether or not he changed their "way of thinking about urbanism" or their architecture, there are so many who have received at least part of their knowledge from Le Corbusier.

Grandeur is in the Intention

Anthony Eardley

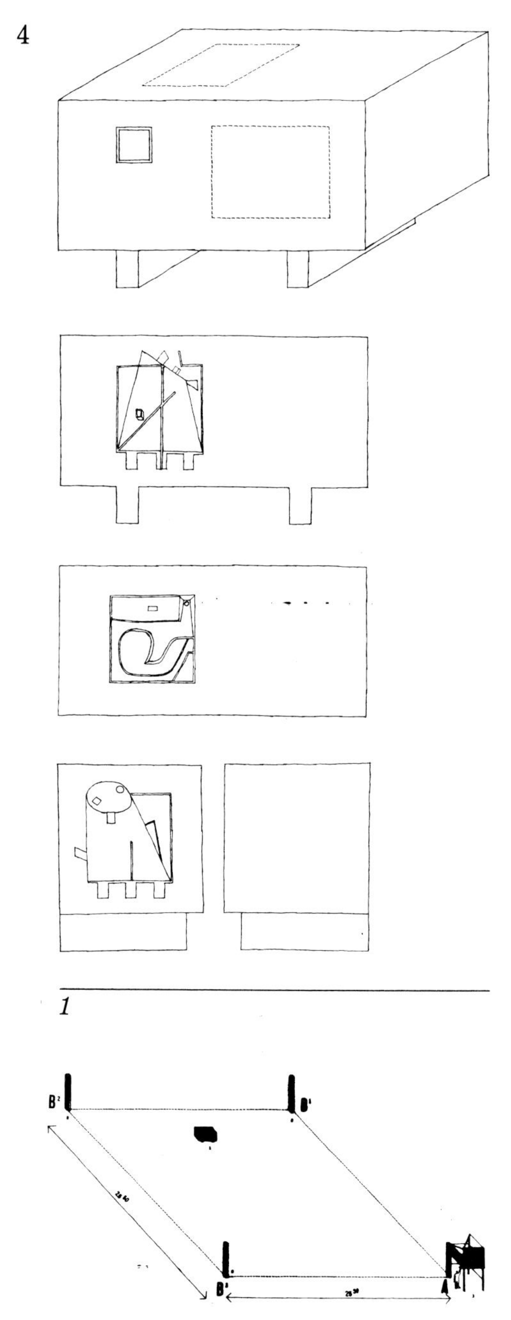

1

2

Firminy is a mining, steel, and textiles town of some 25,000 people in the southern Auvergne. It lies in an undulating landscape at the head of a narrow region sprawling from the Rhone through St. Etienne, blackened with smoke and soot, and containing some half a million people. In the nineteenth century it was the scene of feverish industrial activity. In 1914 Baedeker's guide to *Southern France* afforded Firminy's urban and architectural heritage just two lines of text; the remaining two lines advised the visitor as to the means of transportation to somewhere else.[1] However, it is not this jerey-built and unsanitary old fabric, shaken by mining subsidence and reduced to rubble in the frenzy of European postwar urban renewal, but rather the adjacent "green" Firminy which contains the last of Le Corbusier's buildings to be realized, the parish church of Saint-Pierre de Firminy-Vert.[2]

This last work was actually commissioned in the spring of 1960. Le Corbusier undertook it with reluctance, and serious misgivings, which were overcome only through his deep friendship for the mayor of Firminy, Eugène Claudius-Petit. Indeed, even the Parish Association commissioned the work with some apprehension, for despite the encouraging impetus of the radical transformations suddenly taking place about them in a town which had been "practically abandoned by municipal officials of every political color for half a century,"[3] they found themselves ill-equipped to assume the burdens of patronage for a major architectural enterprise. It was also looked upon with thinly concealed distrust by the conservative ecclesiastical hierarchy of the Diocese of Lyon, who correctly anticipated that it would represent the Mother Church in too obdurately antique and incarnate a form, and in fact, its fate has become a matter of indifference to the new left in the Church, for whom the separation of the sacred from the profane by means of ecclesiastical monuments would seem quite peripheral to the critically pressing crusade for a new world social conscience and political morality.

Nevertheless, the cornerstone (figs. 1, 2) was finally laid on the intended site on March 28, 1970.[4] Today, ten years later, the building stands some thirty feet out of the ground with about two-thirds of the concrete in place, almost seventy feet short of its projected dome—incomplete, seemingly abandoned (fig. 3), more closely resembling the ruins of the Telesterion (fig. 4) at Eleusis or the sixth-century basilica of St. John at Ephesus than the new and gleaming contribution to the great white churches of France which its protagonists have so earnestly intended it to be. It owes its halting progress toward this end to the generosity of the local faithful, to a number of industrialists, to artists such as Sonia Delaunay, Jean Dubuffet, Félix Labisse, Alfred Manessier, and Victor Vasarely, and to a few architects also.[5] But it has chiefly been dependent on the continuous dedication of two men: Eugène Claudius-Petit, cabinetmaker and professor of design, hero of the Resistance, Deputy to the National Assembly, Minister of Reconstruction and Planning, and Mayor of Firminy from 1953 to 1971; and José

1 Firminy Church, March 5, 1970. Atelier Jose Oubrerie. Cornerstone. China ink, draft paper. 28 × 20 1/4.

2 F.C., March 5, 1970. Atelier Jose Oubrerie. Monument for foundation ceremony. China ink, draft paper, colored paper. 28 × 20 1/4.

3 F.C., July/September 1979. Linda Salee, Teriyaphirom. Model, interior; view of the sanctuary from balcony, fifth level. Wood. 49 × 49 × 59.

4 The Telesterion, Eleusis. Fifth century plan.

5 Phileban solids and a sketch showing their application in Rome. From Vers une Architecture *(1923).*

(All measurements are in inches unless otherwise noted.)

Oubrerie, Le Corbusier's assistant in charge of the projects since work first began at 35 rue de Sèvres in the spring of 1961, and architect of record since 1970.

Eugène Claudius-Petit had originally seen the building of this church by Le Corbusier as a fitting conclusion to the earlier commissions that his old friend had received and was already constructing in Firminy-Vert—first the stadium, then the youth club and cultural center within the declivity of the church site, and then the Unité d'habitation standing apart from the other new housing which occupies the hill above the crater.[6] Now himself in his seventy-third year, Claudius-Petit deems his continuing effort to bring the church to completion as a personal obligation to Le Corbusier's vision and a last gesture towards the city whose people recruited him and supported him as their mayor for almost two decades.

3

The church commission came to the atelier in 35 rue de Sèvres some two years after José Oubrerie had joined Le Corbusier as a young painter who was becoming increasingly disillusioned by the experience of his *Beaux-Arts* education as an architect. This project became his substitute "graduate school" and a vehicle by which to talk with Le Corbusier. To Oubrerie, the church's completion represents a necessary termination and release from an apprenticeship of more than twenty years' duration.

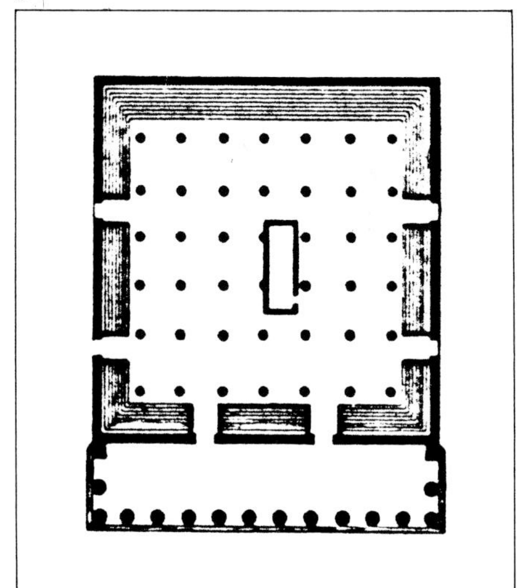

4

Ironically, it is perhaps in its present condition that the church most clearly reveals its classical and eastern ancestry, its primordial roots in the square, the cube, the pyramid, and the circle and the cone (fig. 5). However, until such time as it achieves completion and closure, the dogmatic reiteration of classicist principles, perceived by the observer to be embodied in the stasis of the base, seems to far outweigh its equally consistent efforts to escape the rational, to transcend the rational through the transmutation of cube to pyramid, of pyramid to cone, and of cone to dome. This unbuilt dome, distorted, flattened, and skewed, will become a tragi-comic face, a face upturned to confront a universe and a cosmic force inconceivably more distant, infinite, complex, and powerful than it was possible to give credence to when the engineers of the Pantheon confidently inscribed the oculus in the apex of their last "experimental" dome,[7] or when Michelangelo, working on the Saint Peter's (fig. 6) of Counter-Reformation Rome, dared to group together the square, the cylinder, and the sphere in that "prodigious *tour de force* in stone"[8] which occasioned so much breathless adulation on the part of the young Charles-Edouard Jeanneret.

By the time of the Firminy church the grandeur of these object lessons had been well matched by the Palace of the Assembly, the Parliament building in Chandigarh (fig. 9). No need of vast dimensions for St. Peter's in Firminy-Vert: Le Corbusier's St. Peter's, like its Romanesque predecessor in Firminy (of which on-

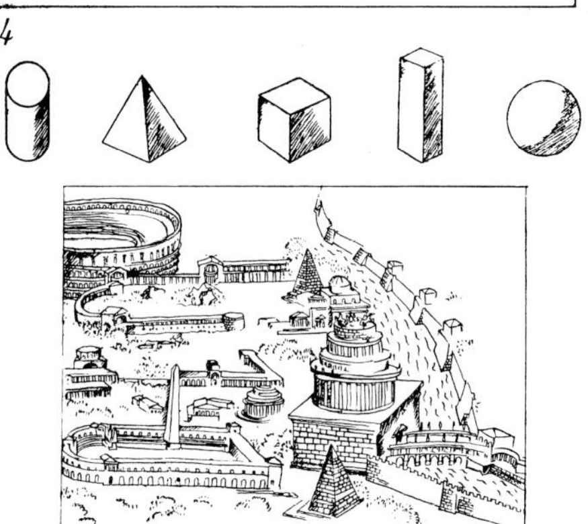

5

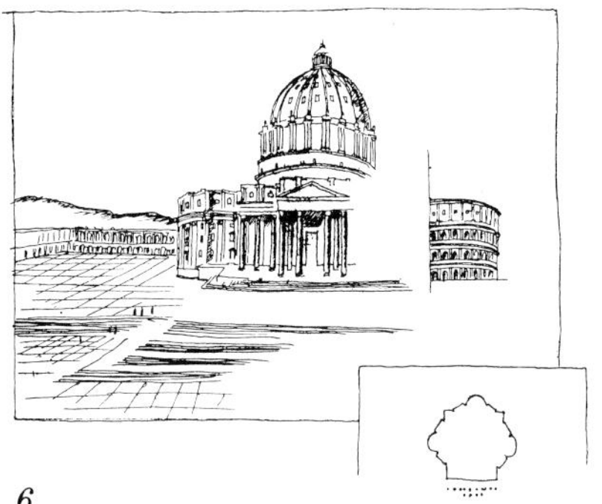

6

7

8

9

ly the doorless portal remains),[9] is a modestly dimensioned parish church, comparatively a very simple volume, raised up and set apart to embrace a small congregation of miners and steel-workers in its silence. And only to this extent may it be seen as an *objet-type*—despite the ancestry of its plan and the eminently prototypical scheme for Le Tremblay (fig. 8), its immediate progenitor, which Le Corbusier first envisaged three decades before Firminy, in 1929.

In the typically sparse language of the accompanying texts to his *Oeuvre Complète,* Le Corbusier said of Saint-Pierre de Firminy-Vert that it: "is, by virtue of its terrain, located at the bottom of a valley. It consists of a hyperbolic-paraboloid shell, and, after Ronchamp and La Tourette, represents a third, new type of church."[10]

This deliberately cryptic and ambiguous statement is almost all that Le Corbusier chose to place on public record about this extraordinary building which, with its elemental program and its single, compelling mass, asserts the presence of a temple on an inverted and imploded Acropolis—a vast, surface-mined crater carved into a hill slope beneath the gaze of the new vertical garden city raised up on its perimeter. It was a unique match of commission and site which enabled him completely to fulfill the plastic and poetic program that he had enunciated so emphatically four decades before in *Vers une Architecture,* his, "Three Reminders to Architects": mass, surface, plan. With the Firminy chruch he was able to demonstrate these lessons more directly and more forcefully than had been possible with any previous project.

The master plan for Firminy-Vert had originally anticipated the construction of a chapel on a rounded hummock dominating the new town, but this location was challenged by the city clergy on the sociological grounds that "people do not climb to the church, they descend, like a woman going to market."[11] What they wanted instead was that the church stand at a point of convergence in the new town as a place of meeting and exchange. As a result, a new location was chosen, and the master plan was revised accordingly. The new site area (figs. 7, 10) (now named the Place du Mail) is the area in which the church construction actually stands, in the excavated crater just below Le Corbusier's Stadium.

As the construction and occupancy of the new town progressed, a Parish Association building committee was constituted to formulate the program for the new church and parochial center and to select an architect. Le Corbusier, however, was not the first to receive the commission. Learning that André Sive, of Sive and Roux, the architect for the Firminy-Vert master plan and much of the attendant new housing, was dying of terminal cancer, the building committee, with Mayor Claudius-Petit's approval[12] appointed Sive in appreciation for his work on the new town. The disease advanced so rapidly, however, that Sive was

6 Saint Peter's, 1547-1564. Michelangelo.

7 F.C., September 1980. Atelier Jose Oubrerie. Site model, view looking east. Carved mahogany.

8 Concept for a church at Le Tremblay, May/June 1929. Le Corbusier. Elevation. Notebook sketch.

9 Sketch of cone over The Palace of Assembly, Chandigarh, 1952-1956. Le Corbusier.

10 General plan of Firminy. 1 Church; 2 Youth Center; 3 Stadium.

compelled to give up the undertaking. Faced with a new choice, and perhaps emboldened by mounting local pride in the fact that "the greatest of contemporary architects"[13] was, by that time, already engaged in commissions for the new city, the committee obtained the agreement of Monsignor Maziers, Vicar General and Director of the Lyon Diocesan Office for New Parishes, to their commissioning Le Corbusier to prepare the plans for the church. That the Vicar General's agreement to this proposal was not unqualified, nor that of Cardinal Gerlier, Archbishop of Lyon, is evident from the tenor of the letter with which M. Baud, President of the Parish Association, confirmed the wishes of the committee to the mayor on March 23, 1960:
"We have made it clear to our Bishop that we are resolved to have our church built by Le Corbusier. His Lordship is not opposed to the idea *a priori* so long as Le Corbusier creates a fitting church... He is a prelate who knows what's what and who has in mind a church that is simple in design but beautiful and representative, for the future, of our contemporary architecture..."[14]

The Bishop's admonishment to the parish was clearly made in the light of the clergy's prior experience with Le Corbusier, but what was intended by it was never made explicit. Indeed, the Diocese's objections to Le Corbusier's scheme were continually being reformulated in terms of fresh rationales: in the beginning the pretext was the excessive cost of landfill foundations.[15] When this was resolved (first by the offer of a donation to cover the costs of special foundations, which was rejected, and then by a written undertaking from the contractor to deliver the building for a fixed price), a new obstacle was found in a protracted reconsideration of the site's location, which the Vicar General himself had originally pronounced as being appropriate, proudly demonstrating its logic at a blackboard. Even amid the final demands for both a new site and a significant reduction in the contract price there was never the least indication on the part of Monsignor Maziers or other members of the Diocesan hierarchy that their objections lay rooted in the nature and artistic integrity of the scheme itself. In fact, their studied air of detachment from this issue might lead one to believe that the form of the building was actually a matter of little consequence to them.

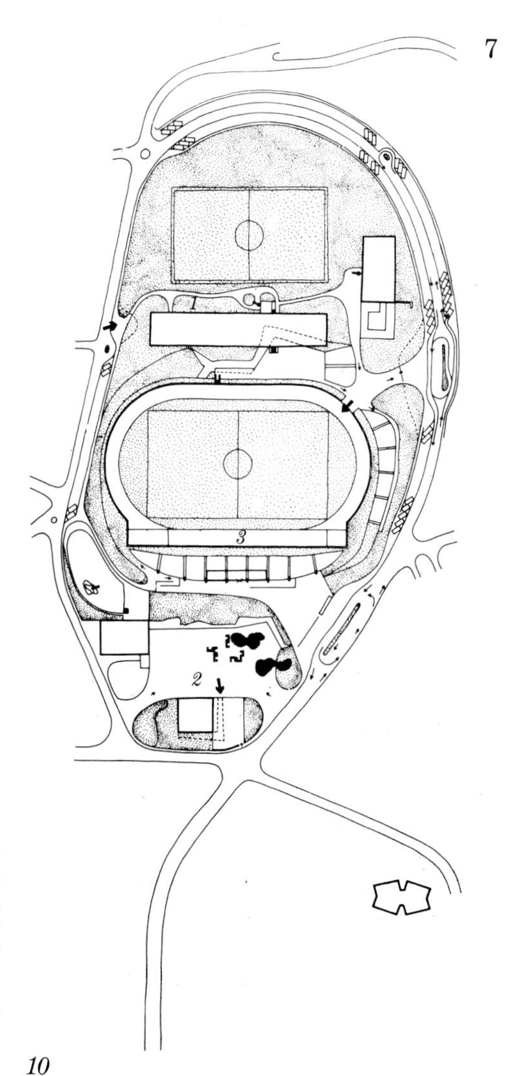

10

1 youth center
2 church
3 stadium

M. Claudius-Petit's introduction to this catalogue relates that he and Le Corbusier had known each other since the fall of 1944, shortly after the Allied liberation of Paris, and that by the end of their American public works excursion together in early 1946 they had become firm friends. He also touches on the subject of his official support of Le Corbusier through difficult, and at times dramatic, experiences in connection with major postwar projects. Thus it causes us little surprise that, on learning of the building committee's desires with regard to its new architect, and sufficiently armed and forewarned by their letter, he decided to pay a visit to Monsignor Jean Villot, recently appointed coadjutor to Cardinal Gerlier, with a view to smoothing out any eventual difficulties "similar to those that have

11

never been lacking in any realization by Le Corbusier."[16] Not entirely reassured by his reception he also wrote to reinforce the wishes of the Parish Committee: "They do not want any pseudo-building; they want something real. They desire neither richness of materials nor technical sensationalism. They wish the spirit to animate inert material and invest the volume, the space, the light, with a meaning. A meditation become reality. They think that Le Corbusier can give them that better than another; I believe they are right."[17]

At the same time, he applied himself to the task of persuading Le Corbusier to accept the commission. It must have been clear to him from the outset that Le Corbusier could be brought to acquiesce and accept such a ticklish commission only with reluctance, with premonitory misgivings which had been honed to near-paranoid sensitivity by a life-time of brave ventures and brutal disappointments, and with an unwillingness to risk, in years of advancing age and failing health, the least time or energy to his last remaining and most precious period of creative production. After protracted hesitation, Le Corbsier finally agreed to his friend's entreaty, but not without some show of querulousness:
"I don't want to involve you in difficulties; I have developed a knack for it! The Archbishop of Bologna has asked me to build some sort of cathedral on a magnificent site on the outskirts of Bologna. I've turned him down. I want to build dwellings, not turn into a church builder. This one at Firminy is the last, and I'll do it because it is for workers, for working people and their families."[18]

Certainly Le Corbusier's sentiment was understandable. The vision of the dwelling as temple of the familial hearth had preoccupied the greater part of his life as an architect and urbanist, and this he reiterated to the end:
"For fifty years I have been studying the simple, good-natured fellow known as 'Man' and his wife and kids. I have been inspired by a single preoccupation, imperatively so: to introduce the sense of the sacred into the home; to make the home the temple of the family. From that moment on, everything was altered. A cubic centimeter of dwelling was worth gold, representing possible happiness. With such a notion of dimension and purpose, you can fashion a present day temple on the scale of the family, apart from cathedrals themselves, which were built...in bygone times...

I for one have devoted fifty years of my life to the study of the dwelling. I have restored the temple to the family, to the domestic hearth. I have re-established the conditions of nature in the life of men."[19]

It was precisely his simultaneously evangelical and pagan joy in sun, space, and verdure which allowed him to boast to his friend Edgard Varèse that he had been described to the Archbishop of Besançon as a true Christian, "but a Christian of 5000 years before Christ."[20] His self-imposed mission as architect-urbanist was

11 Sketch of the Ronchamp Chapel site from the Paris-Bale train, 1951. Le Corbusier. Ink, paper.

12 Soviet parachutist. Photograph from Aircraft *(1935) by Le Corbusier.*

entirely in keeping with the spirit of his early upbringing: he came, after all, from a Cathar family whose Protestant heresies embraced the sun as the provider and regulator of all earthly life; a man for whom a paternal lesson in the miraculous botany of an Alpine flower had appeared a more fitting obeisance than telling the beads of a rosary. And he was to pursue with messianic fervor his vision of an appropriate architecture for a machine era, an architecture which for him was destined to be the fulcrum for universal social redemption. Whatever malaise of the soul might still aflict the athletic engineers and poets of Le Corbusier's new Jerusalem, already raised to the level of demi-gods by comparison with their past urban condition, could well be left to their own innately spiritual attention. Not swayed by, or perhaps even interested in, the anti-utopian prophecies of Aldous Huxley or George Orwell, Le Corbusier took pride in his abhorrence of Futurism.[21] His messianism was derived from his urgent conviction of the rightness of his solutions to urban problems in the here and now. For him, the only plausible Apocalypse was necessarily dependent on society's doubtful recognition of its harmonizers:
"The world lacks *harmonizers* to make palpable the *human* beauty of modern times...
Sometimes in the course of the centuries a man has sprung up here and there, instinct with the power of genius, establishing the unity of his time.
A man!
The flock needs a shepherd."[22]

12

Twenty-five years before the Firminy church Le Corbusier had chosen to illustrate this concept of deliverance with an image of a Soviet parachutist, girded with the most up-to-date equipment, leaping to earth from his troop carrier (fig. 12)[23]. Because Le Corbusier's later architecture exhibits surprising reversals of position and concern with regard to advanced building technology, it is sometimes assumed that similar shifts must have occured in his perceptions regarding appropriate forms of urbanism. All the available evidence, however, would appear to point to the contrary. In concluding the last of his many epistles, written one month before his death, he leaves us in no doubt:
"...I recalled that admirable line from the Apocalypse: 'And in the heavens all was still for a time...' Yes, nothing is transmissible but thought, the crown of our labor. This thought may or may not become a victory over fate in the hereafter and perhaps assume a different, unforeseeable dimension. To be sure, political men fashion their missiles out of any material available and aim at the weak spots in order to attract recruits: they have to reassure the weak and the undecided, the timid souls. But life can be reborn in our plans, potential life in the pastures and the flocks, in these plots of waste land, in these sprawling cities which it will be necessary to dismantle... We must rediscover man. We must rediscover the straight line wedding the axis of fundamental laws: biology, nature, cosmos. Inflexible straight line like the horizon of the sea."[24]

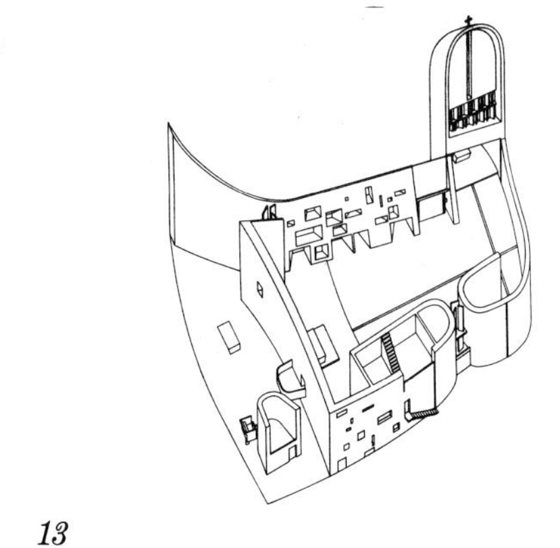

13

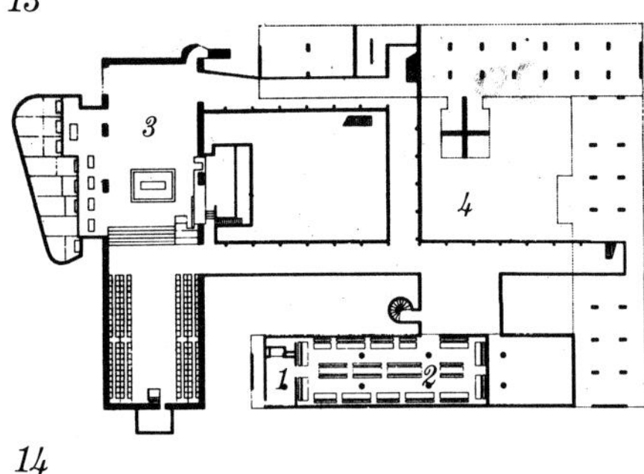

14

1 pantry
2 refectory
3 main altar
4 courts

From such texts we may understand that to accept the program for a parish church would confront Le Corbusier—a self-proclaimed prophet whose parallel crusade was in competition with Christ[25]—with problems of interpretation and even of conscience which the specialized programs for La Sainte-Baume (the "Trouinade"), Notre-Dame-du-Haut at Ronchamp (fig. 13), and the monastery of Sainte-Marie-de-la-Tourette (fig. 14) had enabled him to evade. Something of Le Corbusier's perennially uneasy relationship to the Catholic church may be gleaned from the unfortunate experience of La Sainte-Baume where the client Edouard Trouin had intended to establish a place of redemption in connection with the legendary grotto of Mary Magdalen on the barren, rock-strewn mountainside he owned at La Sainte-Baume. Both Trouin and his idea had strongly appealed to Le Corbusier. In its final form their elaborate program had envisioned the extension of the sacred grotto into an underground basilica in three parts, cut through the apex of the rise and the valley at the foot of the rock. The project included an open air theatre, a museum to house an iconographical collection, a park separating the ancient sacred place from a new, permanent "city of contemplation" built of pise,[26] and two pilgrim's hostels, built in the plan form of "fishing-boats" and intended for construction in prefabricated aluminum. But the basilica itself had been intended as:
"a signal architectural enterprise, an immense, invisible effort expended on the interior, intended to move only those souls capable of understanding. There was no exterior edifice. But within the rock would have lived a work of arhcitecture, of circulation, of diurnal natural light and artificial light, extending from the entry to the grotto of Saint Mary Magdalen on one side of the crag to the opposite slope of the mountain, and opening suddenly into the dazzling light on the limitless horizon of the southern sea."[27]

By late 1948, however, when the project was brought to a halt by the Bishop of Frejus, with the unanimous support of the cardinals and archbishops of France, it was not the rock-cut church but the housing for the "city of contemplation" and the two hostels which had been subject to the most extensive design development. It was no doubt the prospect of building a modern hermitage that most appealed to Le Corbusier in this project, while the whole proposition had its origin in Trouin's concern to preserve his landscape from the ravages of the speculators and the week-end shanty builders from Marseilles, who had already invaded the neighboring Plan d'Aups. In the event, the universal scorn displayed by both Catholics and atheists for the Sainte-Baume hermitage hurt Le Corbusier deeply: "We are at La Sainte-Baume in Provence, a sacred plateau, a 'high-place' dedicated to Saint Mary Magdalen! Centuries of faith. Then oblivion. Then a possible awakening in this era of total ferociousness: tumult, disorder, bewildering inventions, etc... We shall need to be able to think, to collect our thoughts, to meditate. Over the years Trouin and I have prepared a major architectural and iconographic awakening for Sainte-Baume: a subterranean basilica, secret and

13 The Chapel of Ronchamp, Notre-Dame-du-Haut, 1950-1955. Le Corbusier. Perspective axonometric.

14 La Tourette Monastery, near Lyon, 1950-1955. Le Corbusier. Second level plan.

15 Concept for a church at Le Tremblay, May/June 1929. Le Corbusier. Elevation and plan. Notebook sketch.

16 Helicoidal section through Musée Mondial, Cité Mondiale, 1929. Le Corbusier. From Précisions (1929) *by Le Corbusier.*

inconspicuous...and on the outside, the living, living in valid simplicity at the scale of the landscape, at the scale of their gestures and their hearts. It was beautiful! It was a serious and dogged work which had elevated us. But the ill-informed archbishops and cardinals of France cast it under an interdict..."[28]

Le Corbusier's subsequent reluctance to be involved in religious projects no doubt accounts for his initial rejection of the commission for Ronchamp and his negative reply to Louis Secretan, a pastor at La Chaus-de-Fonds, who had offered him an invitation to build a church in his birth place, a gesture which he rejected with almost bellicose vigor during that period in which he first became embroiled in the project for Saint-Pierre de Firminy-Vert:
"I have received your letter of June 20, 1961 asking whether I would build a church at La Chaux-de-Fonds.

"I built the Chapel of Ronchamp (a chapel of pilgrimage) and the Convent of La Tourette (for the inner life of meditation and religious activity) because the program (ritual, human scale, space, silence, etc.) was favorable, as also were the landscape conditions exceptional. I am not a builder of churches, I am continually obliged to decline the offers made to me...

"I cannot envisage myself inserting a church into the context that you have evoked in my mind through your photographs. Forgive me for giving you a negative response. Had you said, 'Will you create a place open all the year, situated on the hilltops in the calm and the dignity, in the nobleness of the beautiful Jura site?' the problem could have been considered. It would have been a problem of psychic nature and, for me, of decisive value."[29]

Be this as it may, the fact is that Le Corbusier finally did accept the commission for Saint-Pierre de Firminy. The site being known to him, he proceeded to unearth the sketches he had made in 1929 for a church at Le Tremblay (fig. 15) on the outskirts of Paris, a scheme in which the elements and the idea of the building type are clearly explored and largely resolved as a strategy, but which for reasons still unknown to us he had refrained from developing at that time.[30] Le Corbusier's renewed attention to this sketch of thirty years before evokes an idea that had become a re-emergent theme in his later work: that of a great central volume, in this case an immensely tall volume almost three cubes high, enwrapped by a climbing processional way, which finally penetrates to the interior at about one-third of the volume's height above ground. Such a basic theme is also to be found in the processional approach to Le Corbusier's beloved Acropolis and, visually at least in the ascending plateau system of the Mesopotamian ziggurat, to which Le Corbusier made direct reference, also in 1929, with his proposal for a museum of world knowledge in Geneva, a *Musée mondiale (fig. 16)* in which the galleries climbed through a great square spiral form to culminate at the apex, which was to contain

15

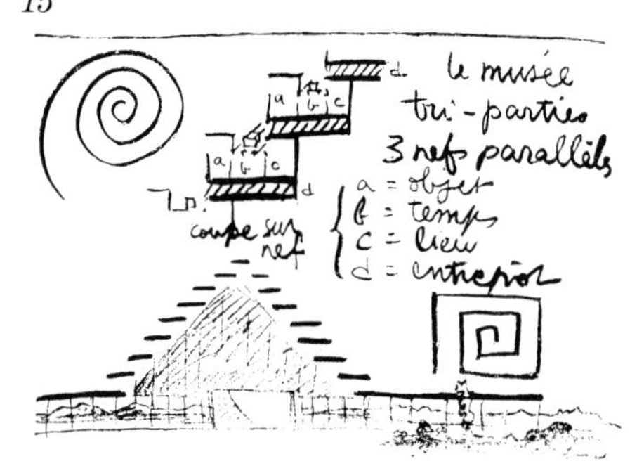

16

17

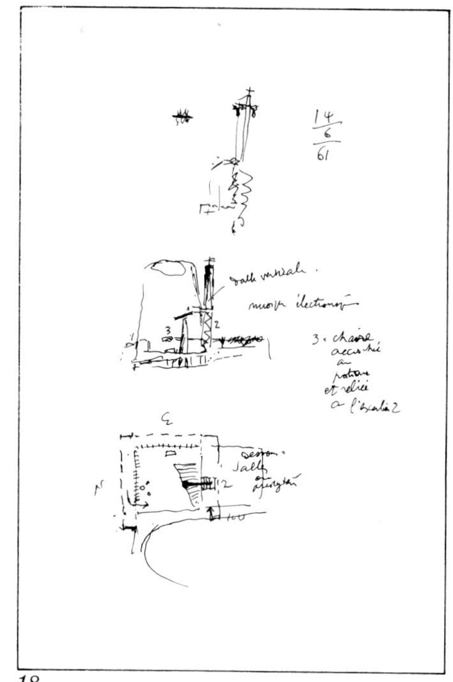

18

19

the evidence of the origins of man. This scheme, strongly attacked at the time for its anti-functionalist formalism, was soon after rationalized and generalized into the horizontal square spiral of the *Musée à croissance illimitée,* upon which his museums in Ahmedabad (1954-1957), Tokyo (1957), and Chandigarh (1964) were eventually to be based. Instances of an abiding interest in the pyramidal compositional theme are to be found in several places in Le Corbusier's work, and an actively renewed attention to the spiral promenade climbing around a vast vertical volume occurs almost a decade prior to the Firminy church commission. Thus, in his first thoughts for the Parliament building at Chandigarh in June 1953, he conjured a great hyperbolic-paraboloid Assembly chamber akin to the majestically evocative forms of machine-age Ahmedabad's cooling towers (fig. 17) (the grotesque irony of such an adaptation could not have escaped him) with a ramp winding up to an oblique cap tilted toward the sun. As the scheme developed, the ramp was replaced by an independent service lift which then gave access to the roof of the Assembly Chamber by means of a steel footbridge. But the oblique cover to the Assembly shell remained intact, and became increasingly elaborated with sculptural forms which, as Stanislaus von Moos has observed, are reminiscent of the observatories of Jaipur and Delhi.[31] Le Corbusier himself described it as: "a veritable physics laboratory intended to ensure the interplay of natural lighting, artificial lighting, ventilation, and acoustic-electronic mechanisms. Moreover, this framework will lend itself to possible solar festivals recalling to men, once a year, that they are children of the sun, something entirely forgotten in our unfettered civilization, crushed by absurdities particularly in architecture and urbanism."[32]

He had apparently wished to develop a mechanism for controlling the natural lighting so that on Republic Day a shaft of light would descend to illuminate a column of Asoka placed on the speaker's rostrum; but having made a number of calculations, he abandoned the idea, and the roof now contains fixed skylights.[33]

Presumably as a result of this experience, but also quite clearly because such an overt celebration of the sun in a church dedicated to the Christian god would necessarily be received as an intolerably offensive pagan gesture by a Catholic congregation, the oblique roof at Firminy is a much subdued version of that in the Chandigarh Assembly. Nor was access to the roof ever conceived as the magnified event that it is at Chandigarh; there was never quite as much of a processional way to a rooftop physics laboratory, and in the final scheme even the matter of service access is still somewhat problematical. But the cruciform incision admitting perhaps too generous or too unmysterious a light to the interior, which we find in the earliest scheme for the roof (EG FIR 5758) (figs. 5, 18, 19), was quickly superseded by another light box—the two *canons à lumière* in the final project having precisely the same intended function as the mechanisms at Chandigarh, namely to illuminate the high altar on Good Friday morning and Easter morning.

17 The Palace of the Assembly, Ahmedabad, 1953. Le Corbusier.

18 F.C., June 14, 1961. Le Corbusier. Section and plan. Ink, paper. 8 1/4 x 10 9/16.

19 F.C., June 18, 1961. Le Corbusier. Study for natural and artificial light. Ink, pencil, paper. 8 1/2 x 10 1/2.

20 F.C., November 1962. Le Corbusier. Sketch showing certain enforced economies: the reduction in the cone height and the realignment of the entry from the ground. Colored pencil, draft paper. 24 1/4 x 20 1/8.

21 Sketch of the menhirs at Carnac, and other generic architectural forms. From Précisions.

Having established the point that the roofscape of the Chandigarh Assembly building is in many respects a kind of flamboyantly attired dress rehearsal for Firminy, we must leave the issue of the use of light in the church to return briefly to its origins in the prototypical scheme for Le Tremblay.

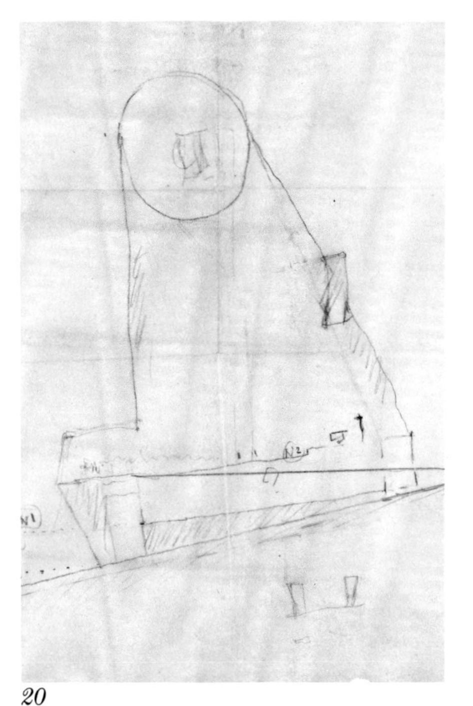

20

For in spite of the many subsequent changes to the form of the initial Le Tremblay proposal, the diminution in height which resulted from paring the building down to the budget (fig. 20), the drastic simplifications of the perimeter, the increasing complexity of the volume, and the detailed modifications to the skin, the initial sketch for Le Tremblay contains the typological essence, the basic approach to the program and plan of the final project for Firminy. But there, I believe, the comparison ends. For if, as a mass, the scheme for Le Tremblay may be seen as a huge druidic menhir, a gigantic tingling stone encoiled in its processional way (fig. 21), of a Purist interpretation of the tower of Babel, then Firminy, for all its reduced stature, must be seen—as it was clearly intended to be—as a mountain or rock standing in isolation, an allusion which is perhaps not altogether inappropriate to a church named for St. Peter. And if the visual activation of Le Tremblay is essentially the outcome of spiral volumetric activity on its periphery, the attenuated spiral promenade of Firminy—its rotation reversed, on entry into the building, by the movement of the warped floor plane in the final project—is not at all the same. The spiral activation has now been transferred to the surface of the shell as an ornamental arabesque articulating the seam between water catchment and light admission, and transformed in the process into an essential feature of the building's elaborate physiognomy.

21

As to the underlying cause and process of these transformations, something may be gleaned from Le Corbusier's response to the editors of the student publications of the School of Architecture at the University of North Carolina at Raleigh, who became interested in the evolution of this project as early as 1964. On this occasion Le Corbusier wrote:

"To publish the sketches of the birth of an architectural work may be interesting.

"When a task is entrusted to me, it is my habit to put it *in the interior of my memory,* that is to say, to permit myself no sketch for some months. The human head is so made that it possesses a certain independence: it is a box into which one can toss the elements of a problem. Let them 'float,' 'simmer,' 'ferment.' Then one day, out of a spontaneous initiative of the inner being, it clicks: one takes a pencil, a piece of charcoal, colored crayons (color is the key to the proceedings), and one gives birth on the paper: the idea comes out—the child is delivered, it has come out into the world, *it is born.*

"Jose Oubrerie made the drawings."[34]

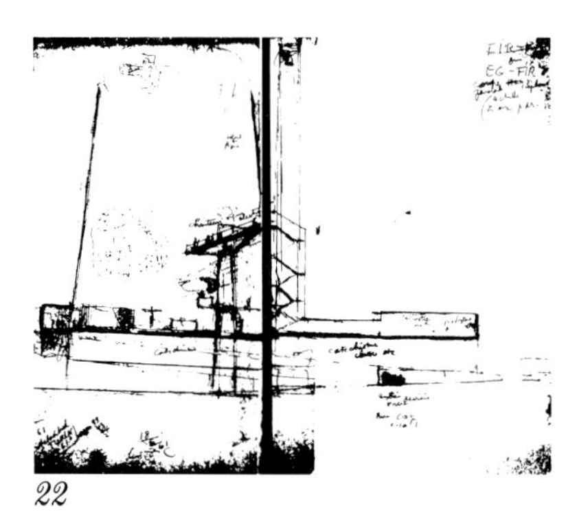

22

23

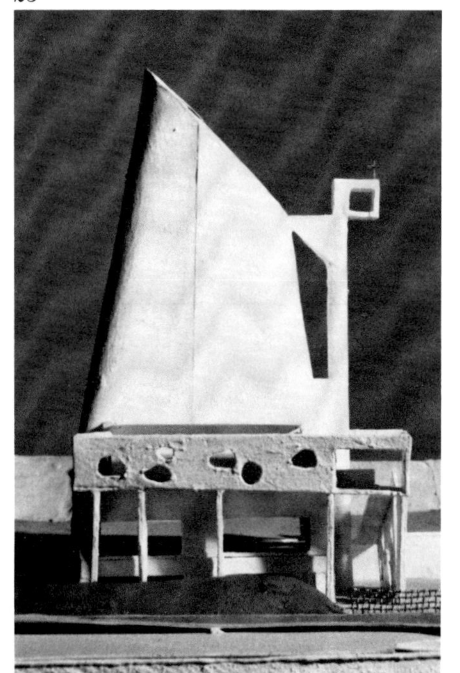

24

The first plan and sectional studies (figs. 22, 25) provided to Oubrerie by Le Corbusier on June 10, 1961 in order to amplify the Le Tremblay sketches indicate several major departures from the original form of the idea. The triple cube has been shrunk in height and its volume progressively reduced into the truncated conic pyramid with which we are now familiar. The spiral promenade is reduced from a complete circumnavigation of the building to a climb along only the east and north walls, with entry to the church being located in the west corner of the north wall. From this point of entry, the immediate view of the altar is obstructed by the curvilinear walled enclosure containing the baptistry. On the south side, a pavilion containing the sacristy, presbytery, and Sunday school classrooms has been pulled out from the base, the link to the pavilion also providing access to a staircase which doglegs around the tower half of a tall vertical cantilever supporting a belfry— the only assertion of the vertical in the scheme—until it reaches the mid-height of the building, where its landing penetrates the shell. This gives access to the upper edge of a choir and organ gallery tilted toward the north—away from the altar—and dizzyingly poised, as it were, in the treetops of the space. This gallery is supported independently by a single massive column which, to sustain it, thrusts up, tree-trunklike from the ground, through the floors of the parochial center and then on into the church, arriving in the middle of the congregation seating area. In the plan there is some indication of hesitancy over how much of the floor area should be assigned to seating. This same tree-trunk provides support to a pulpit which is cantilevered from it directly over the heads of the seated faithful. A small staircase clings to the side of the trunk to give access to the pulpit from the floor of the church. A "rose window," the largest aperture in the shell, is placed eccentrically in the northern half of the east wall of the church, roughly in line with the cruciform roof light in the dome. The promenade to the church and the location of the elements within would seem to reinforce a continuous rotation, which finally climbs to the skylight in the dome. The only static element is the altar, stabilized by its axial centrality beneath the east wall (fig. 23).

Within a few days of these initial sketches on June 14, 1961, Le Corbusier revised the idea. The outer wall of the access promenade is now perforated with generous curvilinear openings, akin to those in the covered connecting passage between the Chandigarh Secretariat and the Assembly building, while the lower portion of the east and north walls of the shell has been subjected to an implausibly high degree of structural erosion to permit a view from the church to the ramp and to borrow light from the new openings in its outer wall. By this means, strong patches of east light would infuse the volume from behind the altar during the morning masses, while a heavily baffled north light would allow at least some visiblility throughout the day. This new system of daylighting appears to have been seen as a possible alternative to the rose window, which would clearly threaten the integrity of the shell with difficult structural problems. The baptismal font has been stripped of its enclosure and pushed closer to the eroded shell wall to free the

22 F.C., June 6, 1961. Le Corbusier. Basic section. 15 7/16 x 12 5/8.

23 F.C., November 1961. Jose Oubrerie at Atelier Le Corbusier. East and south facades.

24 F.C., October 28, 1962. Jose Oubrerie at Atelier Le Corbusier. Model, west facade.

25 F.C., October 28, 1961. Le Corbusier. Porch and entry study. Notebook sketch; pencil, paper. 5 3/8 x 11 7/8.

space and permit a view of the altar from the entry, and the seating has been firmly reduced from a half to a quarter of the total floor area in a manner similar to that at Ronchamp.[35] The tree-trunk column has been moved slightly closer to the center of the floor area, and thus sits on the periphery of the reduced seating area, while the pulpit cantilever has been extended so as to place it on axis with the altar and somewhere very close to the center point of the plan. On the exterior the presbytery pavilion has been expanded to the point at which its roof fills an adjacent square of the same dimension as the church, and appears to act as a gathering place or parvis between the inclined footpath and the base of the ramp. Though by no means static, the whole composition has become decidedly more stable as a result of these revisions.

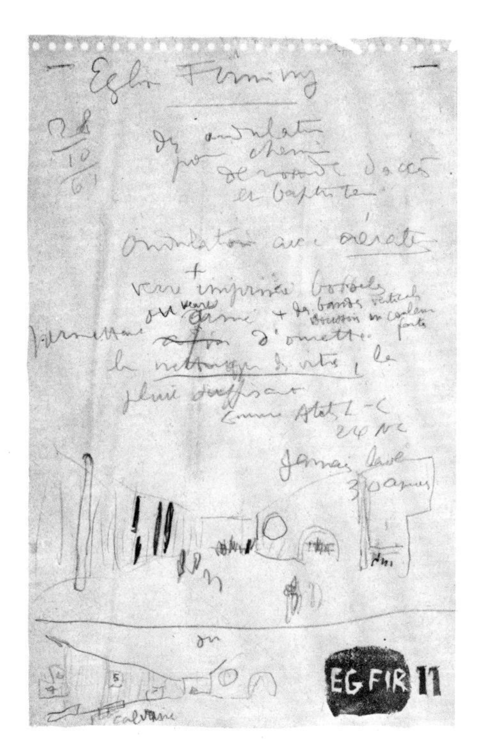

25

Thus armed with his idea (fig. 24), Le Corbusier paid a visit to the site on June 24, 1961. Eugène Claudius-Petit has recorded his recollections of Le Corbusier's trip as follows:
"An entire day in glorious sunshine, with the parish priest [Father Roger Tardy], the chairman and members of the executive committee, accompanied by myself. Sketchbook and pencil in hand, Le Corbusier ranged every direction of Firminy-Vert making numerous sketches of the site area from every viewpoint, tracing the figures of the surrounding ridges and marking the salient masses, recording the buildings already built and inhabited, noting with a word the color and significance of objects. At last he climbed up to the highest point, observed everything with his peculiar acuity of perception, and slowly walked down to the precise spot where he sited the church. An auspicious decision which located the center point only fifteen meters from the place previously chosen in agreement with the clergy." (figs. 26-29)[37]

One or two weeks later, Le Corbusier wrote to Father A.M. Cocagnac, then director of *L'Art Sacré*,
"about a church that I am designing for Claudius-Petit at Firminy. He forced my hand but I accepted because the geographic and topographic conditions were favorable. I have a plan and would like to discuss it with you...to see if you approve of the liturgical arrangement."[38]

It was to the informed and entirely sympathetic priests of *L'Art Sacré* that Le Corbusier had invariably turned for advice on the liturgy, and for programmatic criticism of his ecclesiastical work.

The preliminary scheme, worked out with a somewhat improvised program was presented on October 30, 1961 at 35 rue de Sèvres to Father Tardy, Parish Association President Daud, and the mayor, with Fathers Cocagnac and Capellade also being present. Faults were found with the congregation area, the sizes of the meeting rooms and the rectory, and the disposition of the day chapel in

26

27

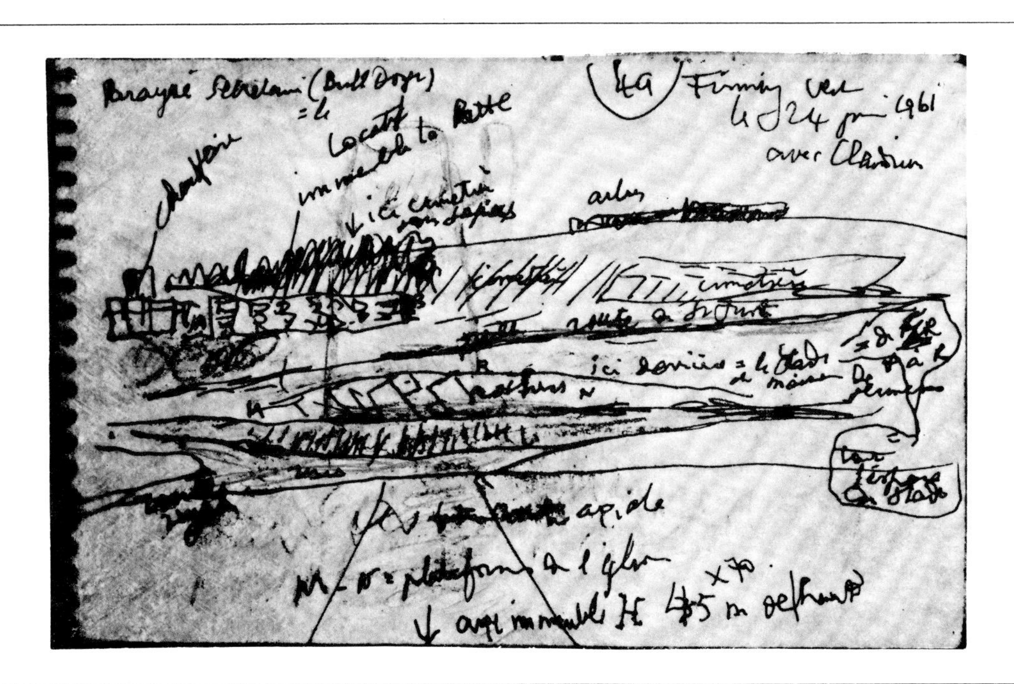

28

26 F.C., June 24, 1961. Le Corbusier. On-site sketch of the Firminy-Vert skyline, view from north. 4 5/8 × 8 1/8.

27 Site visit to Firminy-Vert to determine location of the Church, June 1961.

28 Firminy-Vert, June 24, 1961. Le Corbusier. On-site study, looking from the site toward the east. Notebook sketch, colored pencil. 4 1/2 × 1/4.

29 Firminy-Vert, June 1961. Sketching during site visit.

29

30

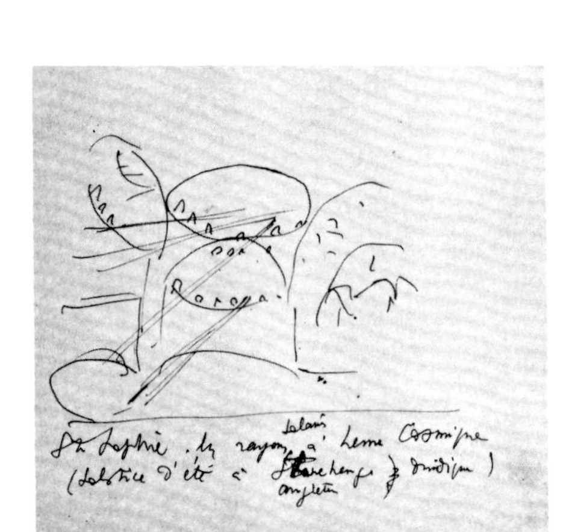

31

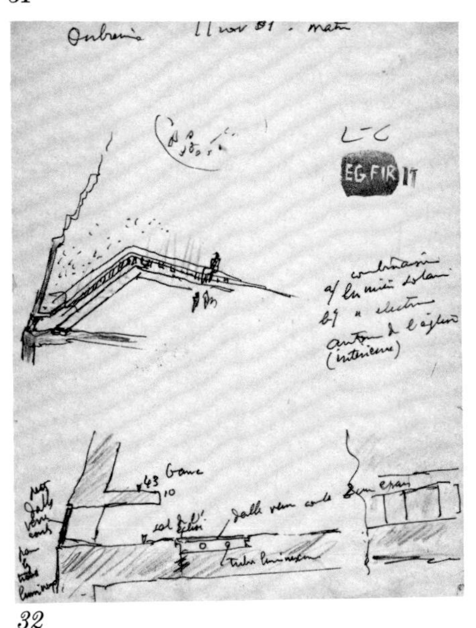

32

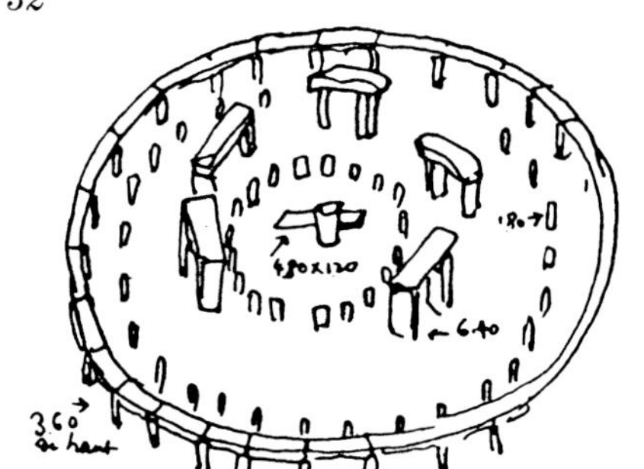

33

its crypt-like gallery, and, finally, the apparently high cost of the proposal. Le Corbusier is reported to have listened with the greatest patience and participated in the dialogue without fuss. At the conclusion of the meeting he asked for a precise program, including the construction budget, with which he undertook to comply.

A quite detailed program was then established, the Parish committee and the religious authorities being in complete agreement on its terms. The budget ceiling was set at what would be the equivalent of ninety-seven million francs today. Le Corbusier set to work again, and after a long and rather arduous process, arrived at the final scheme. Central to the final transformation was the contraction of the parochial center facilities back into the base of the church. One also remarks the diminishing role of the ramp and the changes in its proportional order, the identification of the perimeter daylighting system (fig. 32), at first confined to horizontal apertures at the floor level of the church, the elimination of the choir gallery, and with this, the loss of both the image of the familial tree and the bell tower, the latter being compensated for by the reassertion of the vertical in the north wall of the shell. One further notices the restoration of the day chapel to the main floor of the church and, with the warped seating plane which accompanied this effort to increase the capacity of the diminished floor area to accommodate the congregation attending Sunday masses, the surface activation of the shell by the climbing spiral of the perimeter daylighting, subsequently rendered more articulate by combining the projected gutter system with a *brise-soleil.* This upward shift in the perimeter daylighting contributed to the decision to substitute pinpoint holes resembling the "star" wall at Ronchamp for the structurally tenuous "rose window" in the east wall of the shell. Finally, it should not escape notice that the altar eventually reasserts its primacy by extending downward through the floor of the church to find its foundation in the earth.

The quality of the light was clearly of primary concern throughout the many stages of the design. Given the character of the very first transformations of the Le Tremblay prototype it is perhaps somewhat surprising that exemplars such as Santa Sophia (fig. 31) were not consciously brought to bear on the problem until as late as January 1963. If one looks back to the *Voyage d'Orient,* Le Corbusier's description of the mosques, more dearly remembered even than the Parthenon, reads, not as a specification for Firminy in its final form, but as the expression of its means and intent:
"It must be a place of silence with its face turned to *Mecca.* It must be vast so that the heart may feel at ease, and high so that prayers may breathe in it. There must be ample diffused light, so that there will be no shadow, and in the whole ensemble a perfect simplicity; an immensity must be enclosed within the forms. The floor must be more spacious than a public square, not to hold crowds, but so that the few who come to pray may feel joy and respect within this great house. Nothing should be concealed from view: one enters, and sees the immense

34

square...; no furnishings, no benches, but only a few low lecterns bearing the Koran, before which one kneels; and at a glance one sees the four corners, feels their manifest presence, and builds the great cube perforated by little windows, from which spring the four gigantic transverse ribs uniting the pendentives; then one sees the scintillating crown, brilliant with the thousand tiny windows of the dome. Overhead is a vast space whose form is ungraspable, for the hemi-sphere has this charm of eluding measurement. Vertically above hang innumerable wires; almost reaching the ground, they sustain rods to which the little oil lamps are hooked, a crystalline procession turning in concentric circles, placing a scintillant ceiling over the heads of the evening faithful: then within the girdle of the now faint windows, the interminable wires climb tautly to the underside of the dome and are lost in the obscurity of the immense space..."[39]

Consistently the building became more monolithic. Le Corbusier was born and grew up in the Swiss Jura. From the very beginning his sketchbooks attest to his endless fascination with their changing contours and their contrast with the plain, with the meander of a river, and with the horizontal absolute of the lake or the sea. The single mountain isolated in the landscape or the sea was particularly magnetic to him. It was drawn and redrawn throughout the late twenties and early thirties, as much a part of the *objets à réaction poétique* as were the shells found on the seashore or the shoulder of beef bones recovered from the butcher's meat room. The same excited probing of contour, mass, and texture is to be found in these drawings as was evident in his earlier depiction of the Baptistery of Pisa (fig. 30), a compositional paradigm frequently referred to by Le Corbusier during this same period. Sugar Loaf Mountain in Rio de Janeiro (fig. 34) too became particularly totemic for him. It took on human and superhuman attributes in literally dozens of sketches and in every Rio de Janeiro project perspective for which he could find a pretext.

In this context, these drawings are evocative of a passage from his book *When the Cathedrals Were White:*
"In crossing the Franco-Belgian frontier the train passes through the 'Borinage' mining region. What ever is this, a mirage? As far as the plain's horizons, gigantic pyramids stand out against the sky. I refer to my first trip, long ago. My emotion was intense. These sublime monuments were thrust into the distant blue, to the left, to the right of the train. They were nothing but the coal mine slag 'tips,' waste piles of grey-black schist which had once compressed seams of coal. Now I understand: the rail laid up the side of the slope carries the tip-trucks to the apex of the pyramid where they tip. The law of the landslide determines the fate of pyramids forever: a flawless incline of 45 degrees. And thus I am near to Cairo, in the land of the Pharaoh.

"No, I'm not! Though still intense, my emotion is becoming dulled. My admiration

30 Detail of a sketch made from a train to Pisa, June 4, 1934, showing Cathedral, Baptistry, and tower on the Campo Santo.

31 Sainte Sophie, May/June 1929. Le Corbusier. Pencil, ink, paper. 8 × 11 1/2.

32 F.C, November 11, 1961, morning. Le Corbusier. Study for lighting and bench. Pencil, ink, paper. 8 1/2 × 10 1/2.

33 Sketch of druid site, Stonehenge, Salisbury.

34 Initial project for Ministry of Education, Rio de Janeiro, Brazil, 1936. Le Corbusier. Interior. Figures drawn by Oscar Niemeyer.

35

36

dissolves. These things are not masterpieces, they are not achievements. They are just schist wastes. And now I take the measure of the chasm which may yawn between the aspect of a thing and the essence of the spirit which has given rise to it. The intention is what touches us in the depths of our heart, the essence of the spirit brought to the realization of the work. Here, there is nothing more than an industrial undertaking in which no elevated intention arises. For good reason.!

"And however recent my understanding may be, however simple my soul, well! Here I do not hear the word of a man or of men. A law of physics and an effect is all that there is. The one abiding emotion is the rigor of that law. Nothing more.
"But within me begins the debate: what if men had made such a thing, intentionally, in order that our hearts might be stirred by the intention?
"The train has passed through the Borinage and the pyramids no longer occupy my thoughts...
"As a prologue to the narrative of this first voyage to the U.S.A., under the aegis of the white cathedrals, I feel that everything I shall say will be qualified by the strength and the essence of the intention which has raised the skyscraper, set the cities on end in the sky, launched the autostradas through the fields, and thrown the bridges across the rivers and estuaries. Our heart appeals to other hearts. That is the measure of our emotion, and moreover, size can be depressing, and pyramids of schist can leave us contrite. Grandeur is in the intention, and not in the size.

"When the cathedrals were white, the world was deeply stirred by an immeasurable faith in the action, the future and the harmonious creation of a civilization."[40]

At Firminy, once more in a mining landscape, Le Corbusier resuscitated this debate which had preoccupied him some thirty years before. He returned, in that industrially scarred hillside, to raise once again that which might stir men's hearts by intent.

As and when it achieves completion the church will stand in its declivity, an "imperious monolith" despite its reduced height (now not very much more massive than the Pyramid of Cestius in Rome) still almost of the same stature, in marked contrast to the multi-cellular apartment towers which flank the site and gaze upon its features in the changing seasons. In certain circumstances or light it may take on an aspect of a man-made mountain, its presence echoed by the distant hills. In others it may reveal the awesome visage of an Easter Island sentinel, listening with strange ears to the voices of the universe. Or in yet other light again, its robot-like mass and the pathetic quizzicalness of its upturned face may seem to portray a machine civilization as fallible and as bereft of certitude as the most ingenious of its inventions.

Of the modifications which have occured in the development of the design since Le Corbusier's death the water channel which encircles its base is among the most archaic; it is a ring of eternal return which Oubrerie inscribed to his memory.

37

38

35 Coal schist deposits at Franco-Belgian border. From "Quand les cathedrales étaient blanches" (1937).

36 35 Rue de Sèvres, Paris, 1965. Location of Atelier Le Corbusier.

37 Le Corbusier with model of the Firminy Church, 1962.

38 Le Corbusier and Jose Oubrerie with model of the Firminy Church, 1964.

1. A concise and informative account of the urban transformation of Firminy is contained in an interview between André Parinaud and Eugène Claudius-Petit, "Firminy, Cité exemplaire," *La Galerie des Arts* no.61 (Paris, December 15, 1968), pp.21-25.
2. Since 1968, when the project was resuscitated, construction documents and contract supervision for the church have been the responsibility of Jose Oubrerie, working in association with Louis Miguel, another "ancien" of 35 Rue de Sèvres from the period of the early Algiers projects.
3. "Firminy, Cité exemplaire." *op.cit.*, p.21.
4. Jose Oubrerie, "Presque au but," in *Architecture* no.15 (Paris, May 1980, p.19.
5. Circular by *Les amis de Le Corbusier,* "Achever l'Eglise de Firminy-Vert par Le Corbusier," (Paris).
6. These three projects are recorded in *Le Corbusier...Oeuvre complete 1957-1965,* Willy Boesiger, editor (New York: Wittenborn, 1965), pp.130-135, and *Le Corbusier, the Last Works,* Willy Boesiger, editor (Zurich: Les Editions d'Architecture Artemis, 1970), pp.10-43.
7. Le Corbusier's commentary on the Pantheon and other monuments of ancient Rome is to be found, together with so much else that is indispensable to an understanding of his work, in *Towards a New Architecture* (New York: Payson and Clarke, 1927), pp.154-159.
8. *Ibid.*, pp.164-172.
9. To avoid the cost of repairing the roof, the municipality sold the church, presumably abandoned by the Diocese, to demolition contractors. See the circular by *Les Amis de Le Corbusier,* "Pourquoi et comment Le Corbusier apporta une architecture authentique a Firminy, Ville ouvrière" (Paris).
10. *Le Corbusier...Ouevre complete 1957-1965,* p.137. All translations other than this quote are by the author unless otherwise noted.
11. Eugène Claudius-Petit, "Note sur L'implantation de St. Pierre de Firminy-Vert" (3 May 1966), pp.1-2. Typescript.
12. The municipality had declared its intention to donate the church site to the Parish Association for a token franc providing it was consulted on the choice of the architect. *Ibid.*, p.2.
13. Prior to the modest commission for the stadium, Le Corbusier's involvement in the development of Firminy-Vert had been confined to incognito visits to provide M. Claudius-Petit with advice. It was his old friend's opinion that the populace was not yet ready for the architecture of Le Corbusier at the time when work on the development plan began in the early 1950s. The scope and ambition of the mayor's redevelopment proposals were of such astonishing proportions that, quite clearly, he might risk the loss of bureaucratic and popular support for the plan if he were to unduly antagonize municipal officials by adding unnecessary controversy to a condition which, one suspects, it had already discovered to be painfully unlethargic. Eventually, all of Firminy took pride in the fact that Le Corbusier had accepted the stadium commission, not least the local architects, who took his presence among them as evidence that he found their architecture agreeable to him. "Firminy, Cité exemplaire," *op. cit.*, p.22.
14. Eugène Claudius-Petit, "Firminy-Vert," in *Le Corbusier: The Last Works, op. cit.*, p.10.
15. On completion of the surface mining, the site had been rented from the coal company by the municipality and used as the city dump for many years. Two unmined ridges provide support for the stadium and the Youth Club and Cultural Center, while the soccer practice field at the east end of the crater, the stadium field in the center, and the church area at the west end are all quite deeply filled excavations.
16. "Note sur l'implantation," *op. cit.*, pp.2-3.
17. Eugène Claudius-Petit. "Firminy-Vert," *op. cit.*, p.10.
18. "Note sur l'implantation," *op.cit.*, p.3.
19. Le Corbusier, *Mise au point* (Paris: Editions Forces-Vives, 1966), pp.31,32,48.
20. Le Corbusier, Letter to Edgard Varèse in New York, 21 January 1954. Quoted by Martin Purdy, "Le Corbusier and the Theological Program," in *The Open Hand: Essays on Le Corbusier,* Russell Walden, editor (Cambridge, Massachusetts: M.I.T. Press, 1977), p.318.
21. "Note. It bores me more than I can say to describe, like some minor prophet, this future City of the Blest. It makes me imagine I have become a Futurist, a sensation I do not at all appreciate. I feel as though I were leaving on one site the crude realities of existence for the pleasures of automatic lucubrations!
"On the other hand, how thrilling it is, before one sets pen to paper, to work out on a drawing-board this world which is almost upon us, for then there are no words to ring false and only facts count.
"Our concern, then, must be with precise inventions, fundamental conceptions, and organisms, that are likely to endure. Everything has to be allowed for at once. Set the problem, arrange it and adjust it, make it hang together, and still keep in mind the indispensable poetry which alone, when all is said and done, can move us to enthusiasm and inpire us to action.
"What I have called an automatic lucubration does not lie in this difficult pursuit of a solution on the drawing-board. It is an act of faith in our own age. In the deepest part of myself I believe in it. I believe in it for the future and not merely because of the formulas that gave the equation, and I believe in it amid all the difficulties of special cases. But we can never have too clear or exact a conception in our minds if we are to solve the problems of special cases."
Le Corbusier, *The City of Tomorrow and its Planning* (London: John Rodker, 1929), p.198. This is Frederick Etchells's translation. It is one of the great ironies of architectural literature that it was Etchells, a Vorticist, who undertook to translate two of the most magnificently atavistic works of the twentieth century, and to transform them into Futurist platforms in the process: *Vers une architecture* became *Towards a New Architecture,* in its title and emphasis, and *Urbanisme,* despite the clear evidence of Le Corbusier's avowals to the contrary, became *The City of Tomorrow and its Planning.*
22. Le Corbusier, *Aircraft; L'avion accuse...* (London: The Studio, Ltd. 1935), p.95.
23. *Ibid.*, p.96.
24. *Mise au point, op.cit.*, pp. 59-61.
25. Paul Turner, in his invaluable study of

The Education of Le Corbusier observes that in his reading of Ernest Renan's *Vie de Jesus* during the period 1908-1909, the young Charles-Edouard Jeanneret marked passages which "reveal the rather startling fact that Jeanneret actually identified himself with the figure of Jesus, and was seeking parallels between Jesus's career and that which he himself was embarking upon... Indeed, Jeanneret seems to have read Nietzche *(Zarathustra)* and Renan together, seeking out in both books the traits of the archetypal revolutionary prophet and reformer—and then relating these traits to his image of his own similar destiny."
Paul Venable Turner, *The Education of Le Corbusier* (New York: Garland Publishing Inc., 1977), pp.62,64.
26. Puddled clay, sometimes containing a pebble aggregate.
27. Le Corbusier: *Oeuvre complete 1946-1952, op.cit.*, p.25.
28. *Le Corbusier lui-meme,* Jean Petit, editor (Geneva: Editions Rousseau, 1970), p.100.
Apart from the secular aspects of this proposal it is clear that Le Corbusier's constant recourse to pagan or natural iconography, as is evident, for example, in Ronchamp, was a constant source of distress to the ecclesiastical authorities.
While it is impossible to identify the full panoply of references and stimuli, it is possible to claim that in addition to the crab-shell and aircraft wing which shaped the roof, other memories permeated the form of Firminy-Vert. Among these one may select the old Greek colony in Archachon, drawn with proto-Purist subtlety by himself and Amédée Ozenfant in the summer of 1918 (Le Corbusier, *Une maison—un palais; a la recherche d'une unité architecturale,* Paris: Cres, 1928, p.47); the Serapeum at the Villa Adriana, Tivoli, already evoked in connection with the light shafts for La Sainte-Baume (Le Corbusier, *Oeuvre complete 1946-1952,* p.31); the megalithic Ggantija (Giant's Tower) on the Maltese island of Gozo (*Une maison—un palais,* p.39); elements of the Arab cities of Ghardaia and the Mizab (Le Corbusier, *Radiant City,* New York, 1967, pp.230-233), and African ceremonial masks which he had studied in the Trocadero in his youth *(L'Esprit Nouveau* nos.21,22, see "Nègres" by Julian Sant-Quetin).
29. "Le Corbusier and the Theological Program," *op.cit.*, p.291.
30. Some indications as to the reasons for his refusal are contained in his response to Karel Teige's criticism of the Mundaneum project of that period when he replied,
"You say 'needs pose programs: factories, railway stations, and not churches or palaces; at the present time, nothing can become architecture which is not dictated by social and economic needs.' I have never believed, nor written anything else; and to show you the subtlety which can animate this belief, let me tell you that last year I refused, very politely, to build a very big church, even though I was authorized to apply the most modern methods to the project. I felt that reinforced concrete simply couldn't become a true expression of a Catholic cult, which is formed by the dense stratification of secular usages which derive their vitality as much from the form that has been conferred upon them as from the principle, and which our memory has retained.
See Karel Tiege, "Mundaneum," originally published in *Stavba* no.7 (Prague, 1928-1929), pp.145-155. Translated in full by Ladislav and Elizabeth Holovsky and Lubamir Dolezel in *Oppositions* 4 (New York: October 1974), pp.83-91. See also Le Corbusier, "In Defense of Architecture." This article was written in 1929 in response to the Teige attack cited above, and was intended for publication in *Stavba.* It first appeared in French in *L'Architecture d'aujourd'hui* (Paris, 1933), and is published in full in *Oppositions* 4, pp.92-108, translated by Nancy Bray, André Lessard, Alan Levitt, and George Baird. My version of this passage differs slightly from theirs.
31. Stanislaus von Moos, *Le Corbusier; Elements of a Synthesis* (Cambridge, Massachusetts: M.I.T. Press, 1979), p.258.
32. "Le Corbusier et son atelier rue de Sevres 35," Oeuvre complete 1952-1957, p.94.
33. Norma Evenson, *Chandigarh,* (Berkeley: University of California Press, 1966), p.82.
34. Le Corbusier, introduction to *The development by Le Corbusier of the Design for* L'Eglise de Firminy, *a church in France,* Keller Smith Jr., and Reyhan Tansal, editors (University of North Carolina at Raleigh: Student Publications, vol.14, 1964), p.5.
35. Le Corbusier had an acute distaste for the clutter of extensive church seating: "They can get down on their knees, the Good Lord is quite entitled to that! Because all these types sit in the churches, including Notre Dame, (and) I don't agree at all!" *Le Corbusier lui-meme,* p.184. In the end, of course, he was to lose this battle at Firminy as a result of the necessity to warp the church floor up and over the day chapel in order to accomodate the congregation in a reduced floor area, thus making safety barriers, and hard seating essential.
36. Several significantly conflicting dates are recorded for the site visit, but I believe we can rely on the date Le Corbusier indicated on his sketches.
37. *Note sur l'implantation, op.cit.*, p.3.
38. "Le Corbusier and the Theological Program," *op.cit.*, p.309.
39. Le Corbusier, "The Mosques" in *Le Voyage d'Orient* (Paris: Forces Vives, 1966).
40. Le Corbusier, *"Quand les cathedrales étaient blanches," Plan* (Paris, 1937), pp.33-35.

Early Drawings
Atelier Le Corbusier 1961-1962

ATELIER
LE CORBUSIER
35, rue de Sèvres
Paris-6e-LIT.99-62

1

ATELIER
LE CORBUSIER
35, rue de Sèvres

2

1 Concept for a church at Le Tremblay, May/June 1929. Le Corbusier. Elevation. Notebook sketch. 8 1/4 × 10 5/8.

2 Concept for a church at Le Tremblay, May/June 1929. Le Corbusier. Elevation and plan. Notebook sketch. 8 1/4 × 10 5/8.

3 Firminy Church, June 6, 1961. Le Corbusier. Basic Section. 15 7/16 × 12 5/8.

4 F.C., June 6, 1961. Le Corbusier. First plan based on "Le Tremblay" concept. 8 9/32 × 13. (Pl.no.5757.)

5 Sainte Sophie, May/June, 1929. Le Corbusier. "Sun rays at a cosmic hour." 8 3/16 × 11 1/2.

3

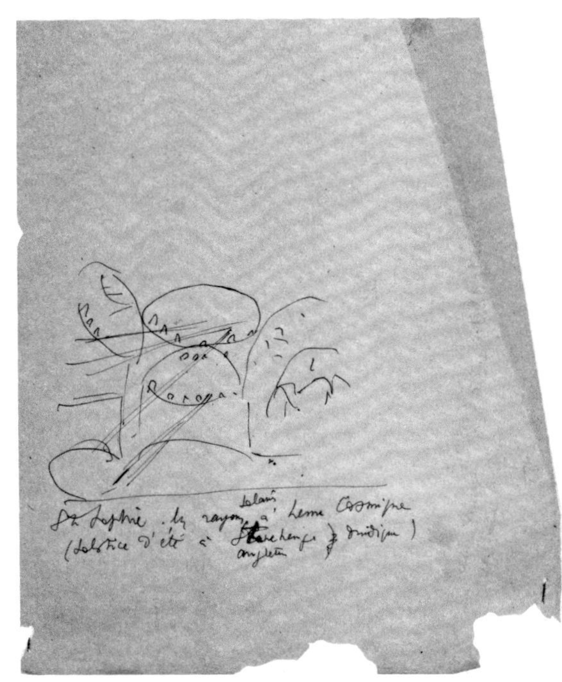

5

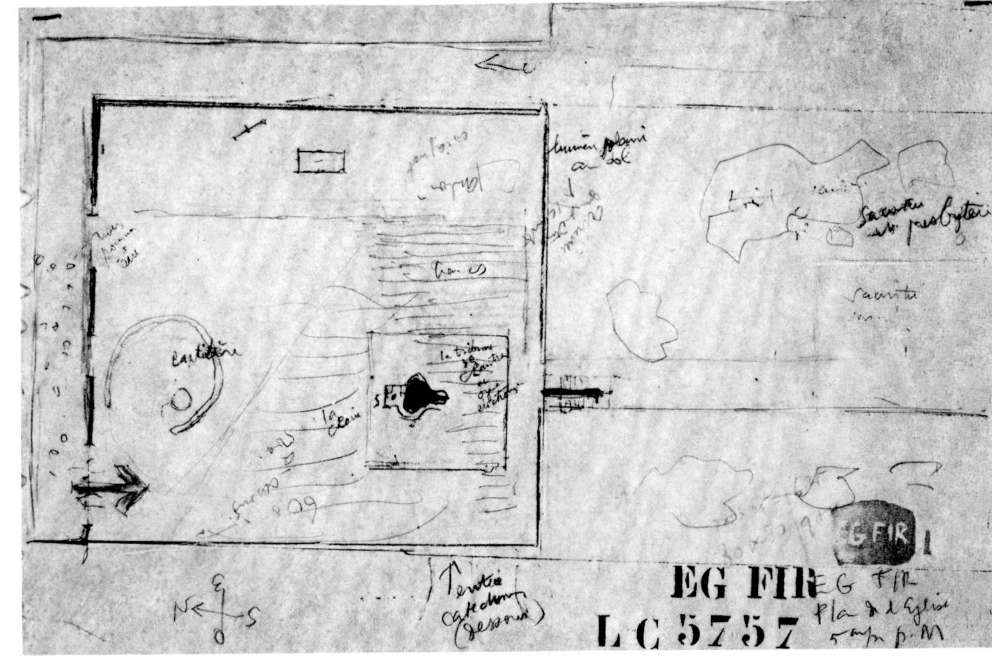

4

LE CORBUSIER

14/6/61

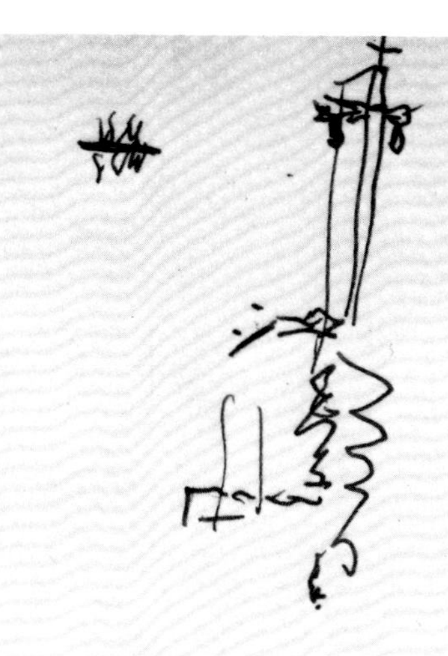

28

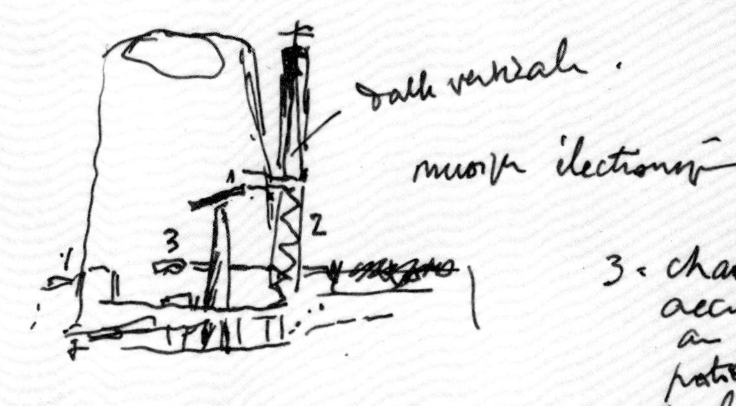

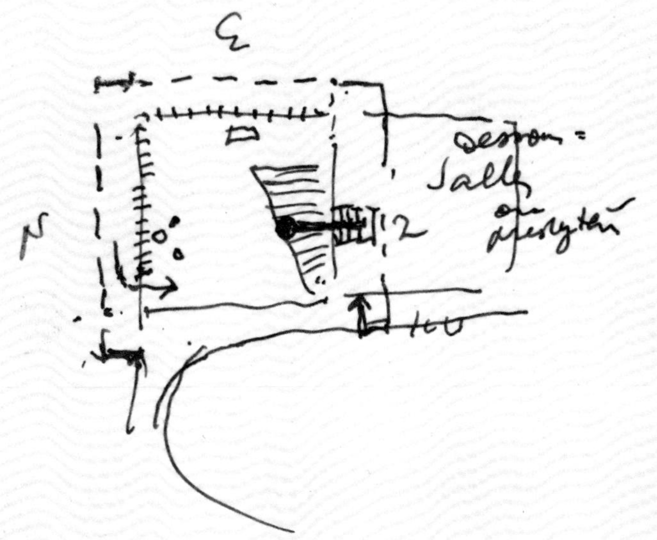

35, RUE DE SÈVRES : PARIS (6e)
TÉL. : LITTRÉ 99-62

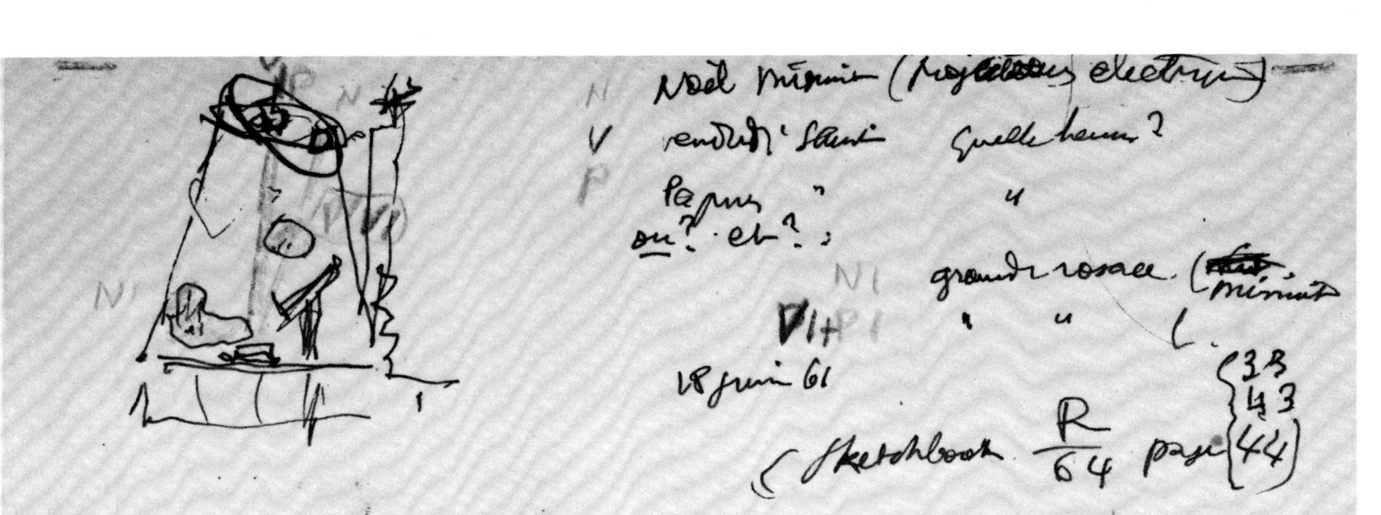

Architectural Adviser to Government, Punjab,
Capital Project.

6 F.C., June 14, 1961. Le Corbusier. Basic concept: Section and plan. Ink, paper. 8 1/4 × 10 1/4.

7 F.C., June 18, 1961. Le Corbusier. Study for natural and artificial light. Ink, pencil, paper. 8 1/4 × 10 1/2.

8

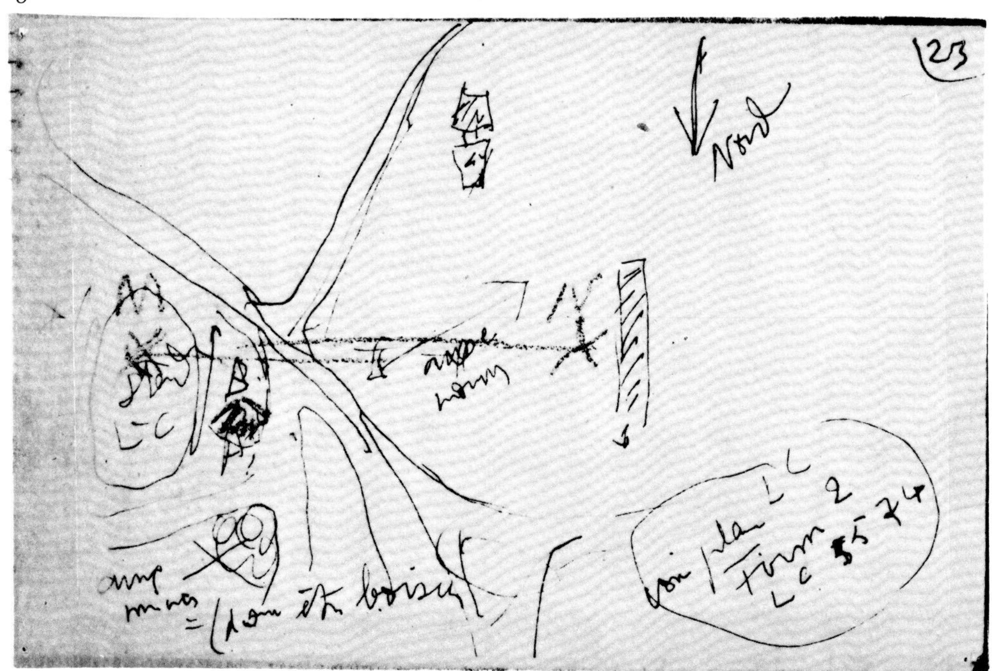

9

8 F.C., June 10, 1961. Le Corbusier. Master Plan. 42×26 1/2. (Pl.no.5756.)

9 F.C., June 24, 1961. Le Corbusier. On-site study; plan. 4 1/2×7.

10 F.C., June 24, 1961. Le Corbusier. On-site sketch of the Firminy-Vert skyline; view of site from the north. 4 5/8×8 1/8.

11 F.C., June 24, 1961. Le Corbusier. On-site study; view from the site toward the west. 4 6/8×8.

10

11

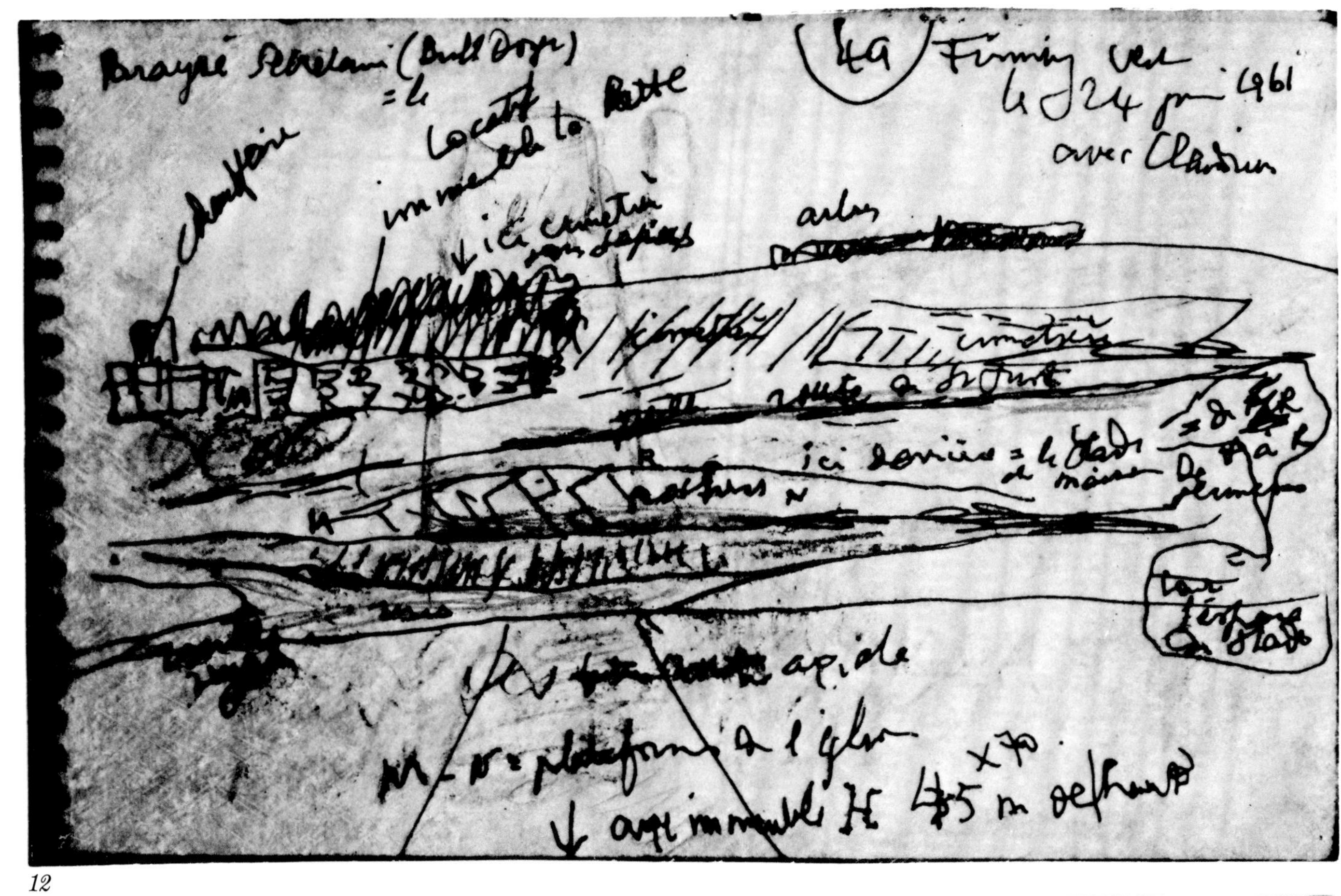

12

13

12 F.C., June 24, 1961. Le Corbusier. On-site study; view from the site toward the east. 4 1/2 × 7 1/4.

13 F.C., September 1961. Le Corbusier. Shell studies. Pencil, paper. 6 3/4 × 11.

14 F.C., July 1961. Le Corbusier. Roof study showing rainwater drainage. Pencil, paper. 8 1/4 × 10 1/2.

15 F.C., September 26, 1961. Le Corbusier. "Le Corbusier climbing with his father." Pencil, paper. 8 1/4 × 10 1/2.

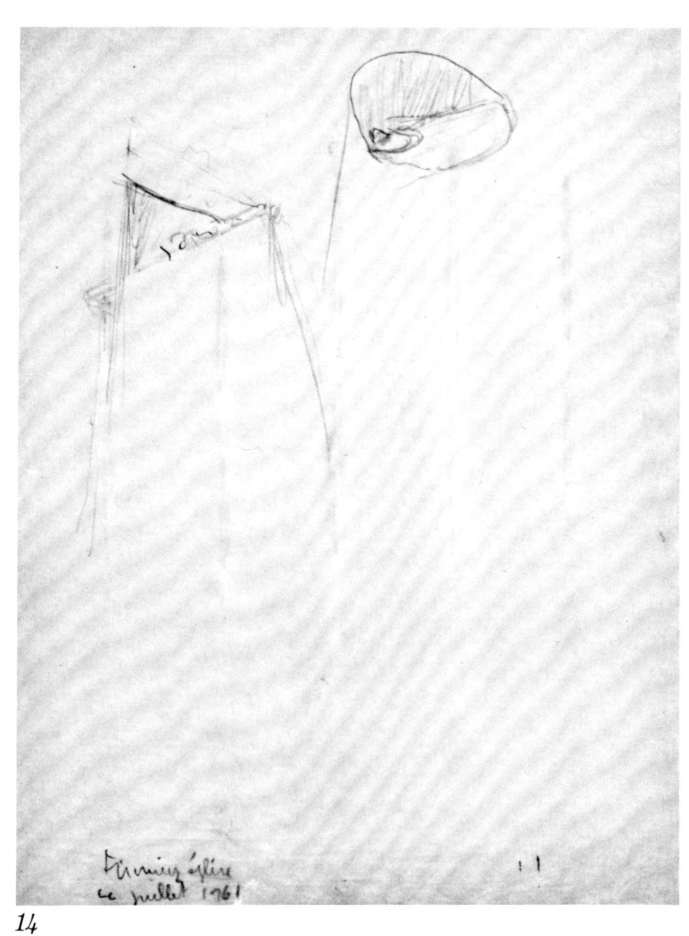

14

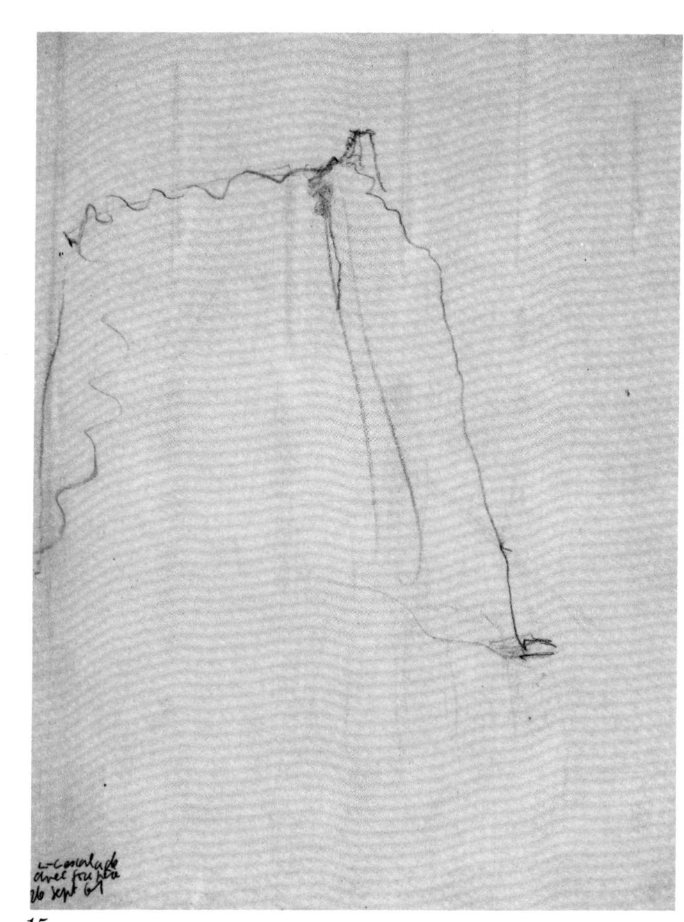

15

16 F.C., October 6, 1961. Le Corbusier. Seat studies. Pencil, paper. 5 1/4×8.

17 Pulpit Study, Reims Cathedral, October 6, 1961. Le Corbusier. Pencil, paper. 4 3/4×5 7/8.

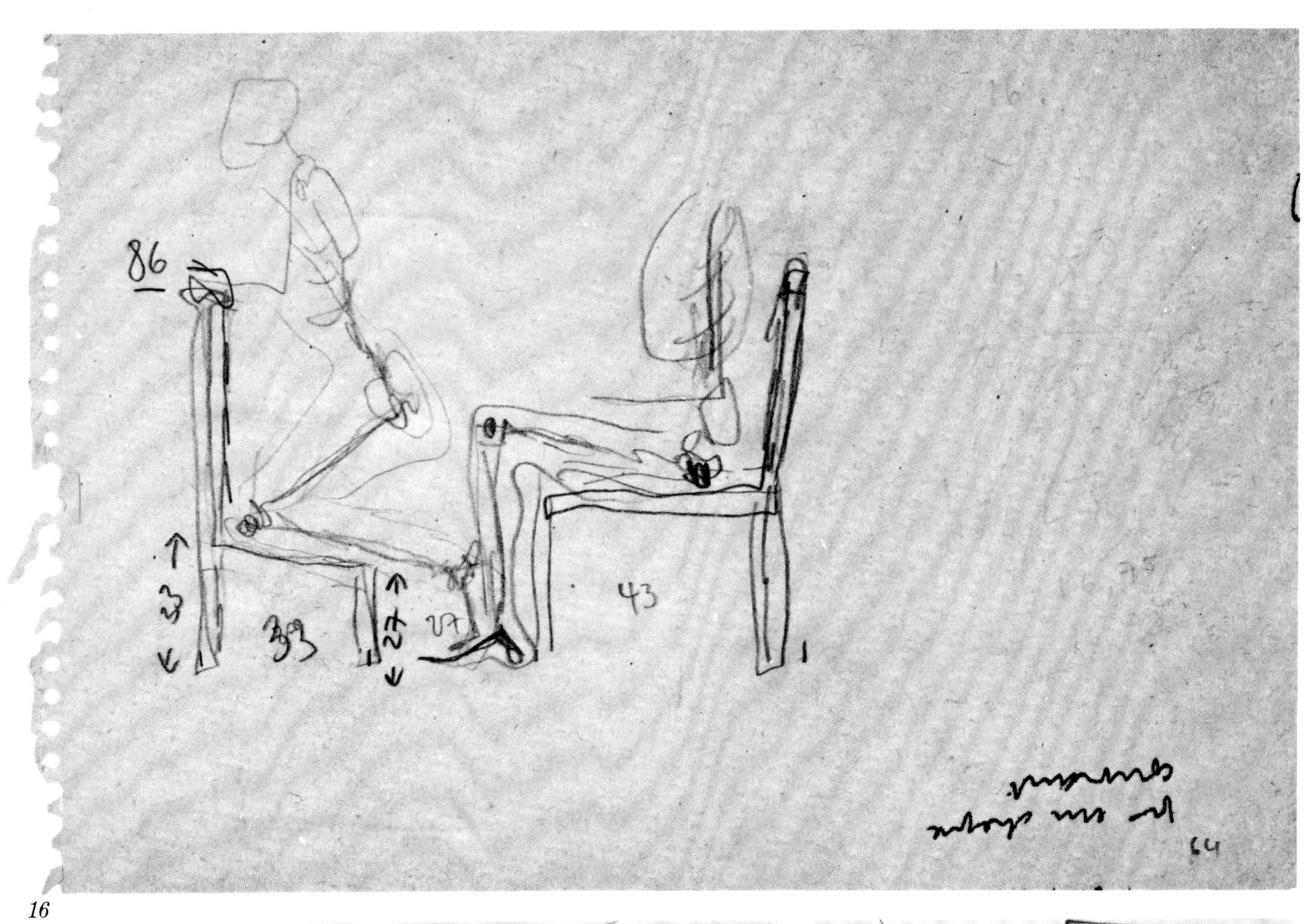

16

17

18

18 Seat dimension study, Reims Cathedral, October 6, 1961. Le Corbusier. Pencil. 4 1/4 × 5 3/8.

19 F.C., September 1961. Le Corbusier. The basic geometry of the Church cut by a plane. Pencil, paper. 8 1/4 × 10 1/2.

20 F.C., September 1961. Le Corbusier. Geometry of the Church and casting problem study. Pencil, paper. 8 1/4 × 10 1/2.

21 F.C., September 29/30, 1961. Le Corbusier. Shell skyline; plan. Pencil, paper. 8 1/4 × 10 1/2.

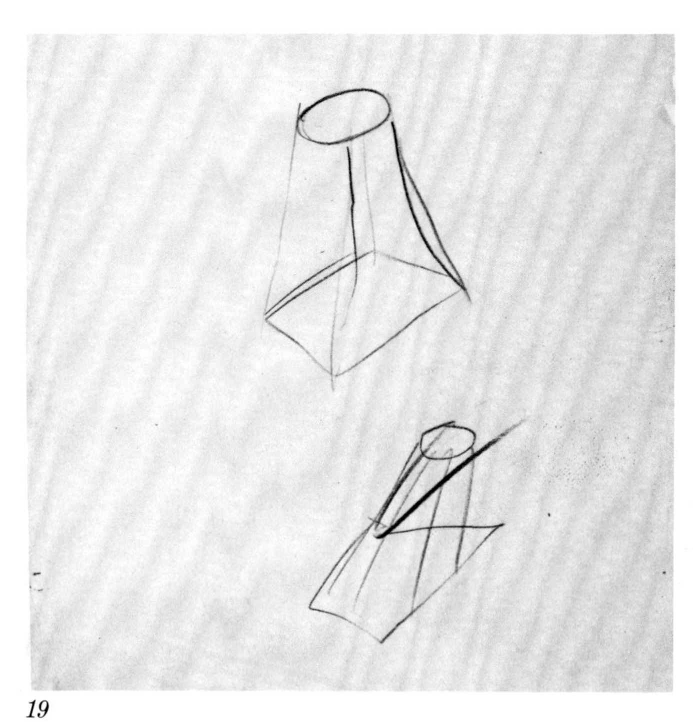

19

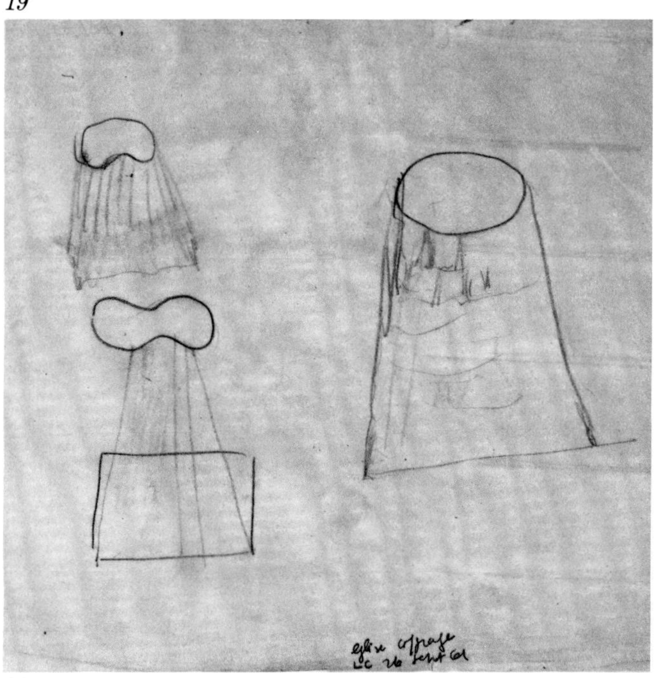

20

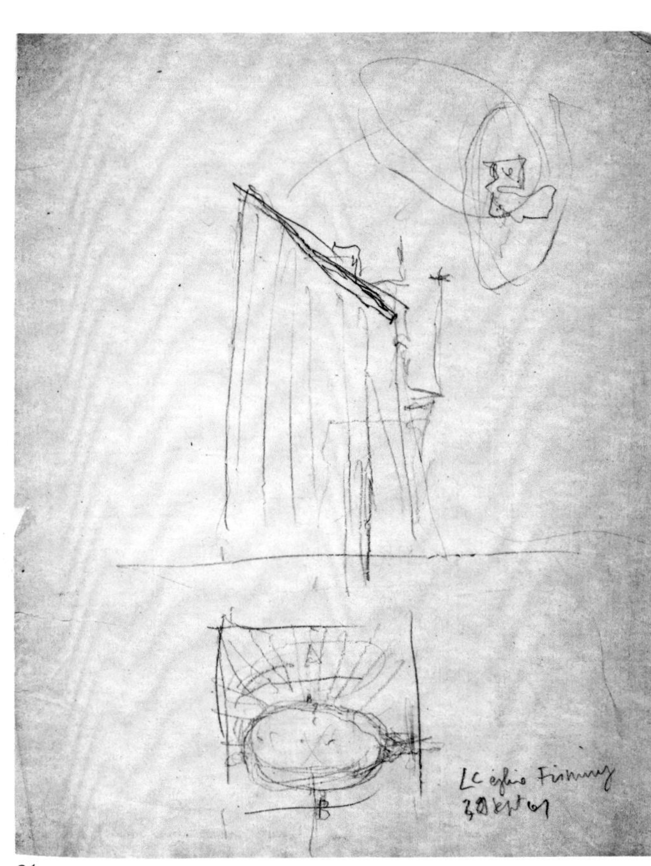

21

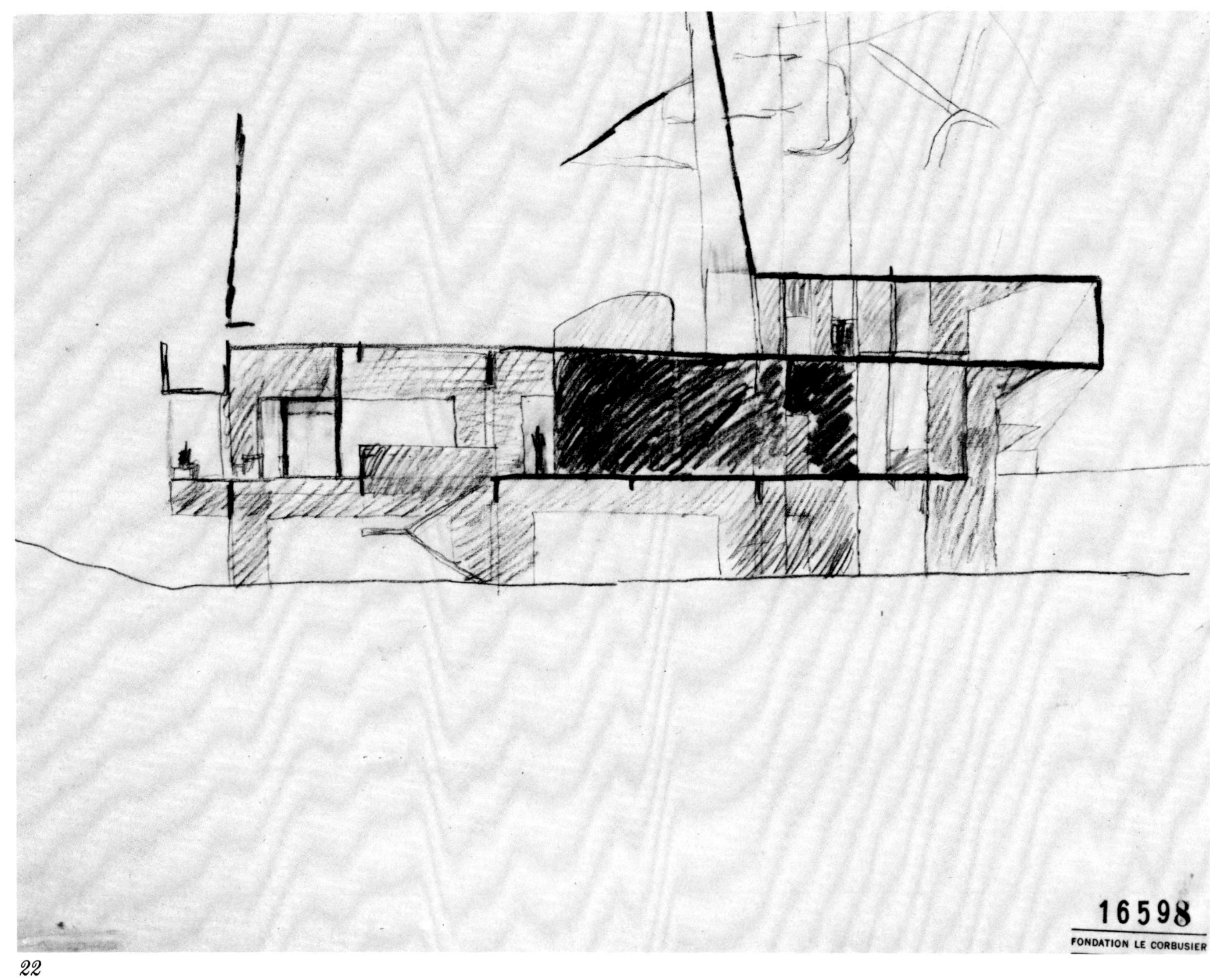

22

22 F.C., October 23, 1961. Jose Oubrerie in Atelier Le Corbusier. Section study. 21 5/16 × 16 7/16. (Foundation Le Corbusier no.16598.)

23 F.C., October 23, 1961. Le Corbusier. Bell tower study. 16 7/16 × 20 1/16. (F.L.C. no.16111.)

24 F.C., October 23, 1961. Jose Oubrerie in Atelier Le Corbusier. East elevation study. Colored pencil, draft paper. 19 5/8 × 22 5/16.

25 F.C., October 23, 1961. Jose Oubrerie in Atelier Le Corbusier. South elevation study. 19 3/4 × 22 9/16.

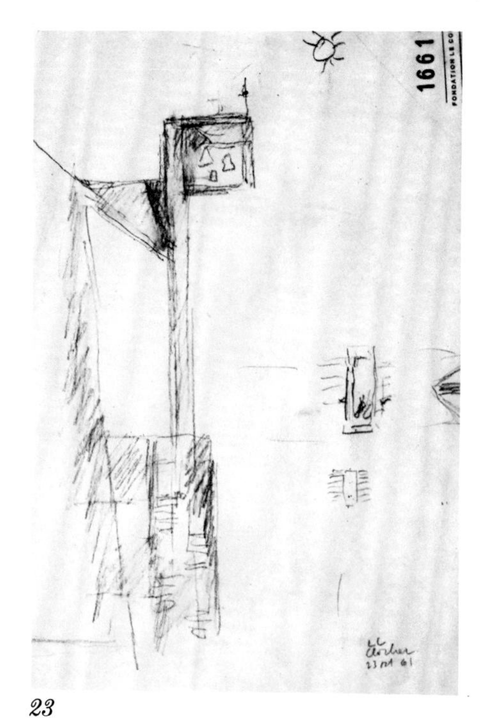

23

24

25

26 F.C., November 1961. Jose Oubrerie in Atelier Le Corbusier. Study plan. Ink, pencil, paper. 21 1/4 × 18 5/8.

27 F.C., October 30, 1961. Le Corbusier. Sketch made during discussion of choir with Eugène Claudius-Petit, Father Tardy, Father Cocagnac, and Father Capellades. Ink, pencil, paper. 18 × 14 1/8.

28 F.C., October 30, 1961. Le Corbusier. Study for pulpit and lecturn made during discussion with Father Cocagnac and Father Capellades. Ink, pencil, paper. 8 1/4 × 10 1/2.

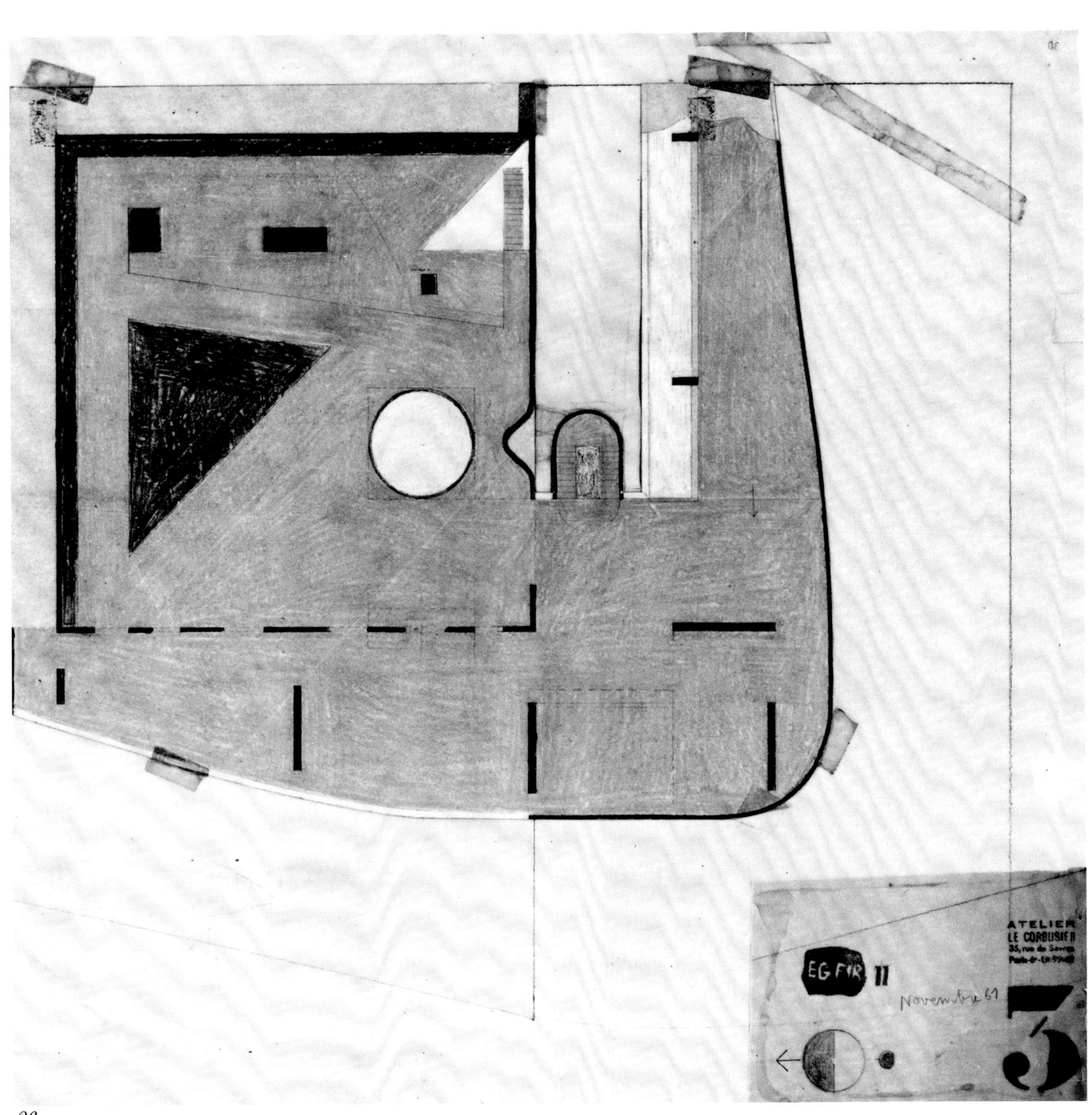

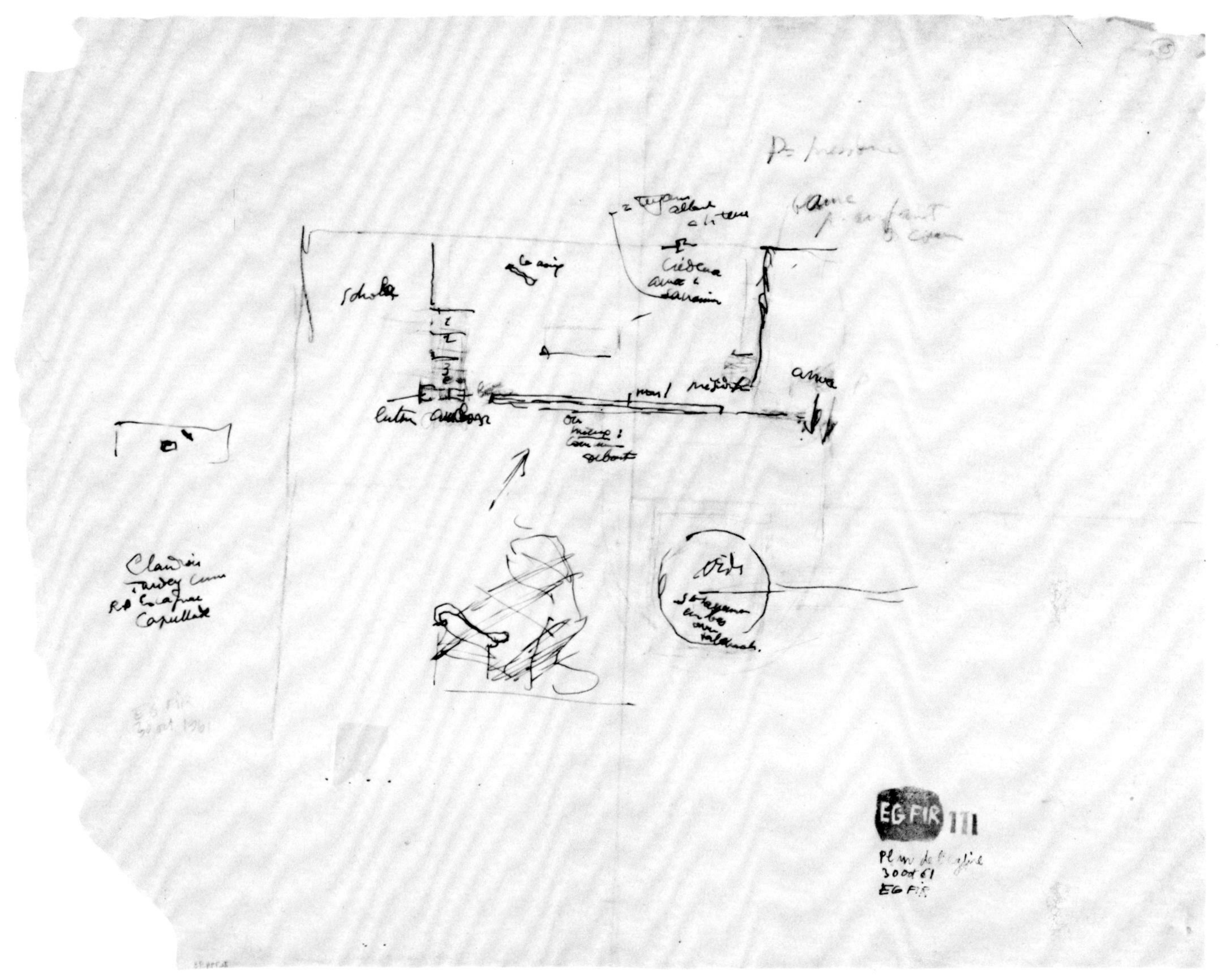
schola
EG FIR
Plan de l'église
30 oct 61
EG FIR

27

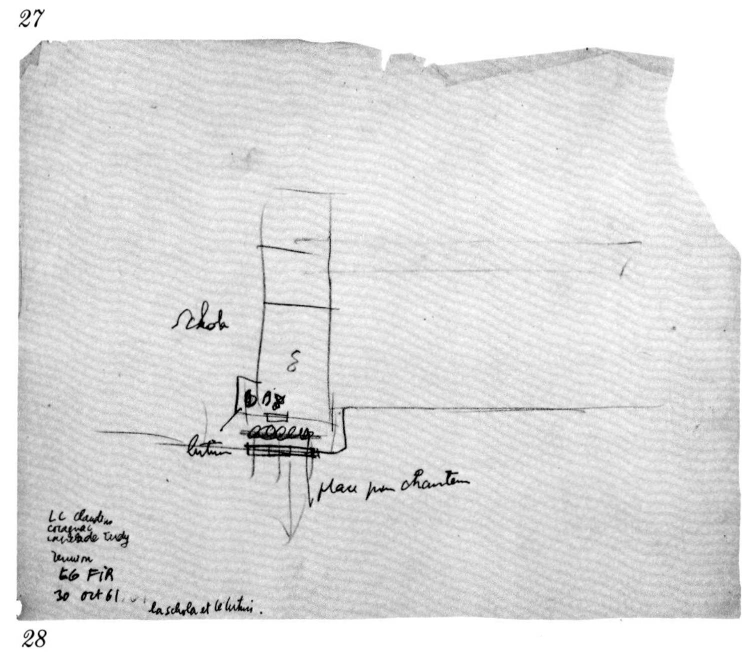
schola
lutrin
place pour chanteur
EG FIR
30 oct 61
la schola et le lutrin.

28

29 F.C., October 28, 1961.
Le Corbusier. Lectern notes. Notebook sketch. Pencil, paper. 5 3/8 × 11 7/8.

30 F.C., October 28, 1961.
Le Corbusier. Porch and entry study. Notebook sketch. Pencil, paper. 5 3/8 × 11 7/8.

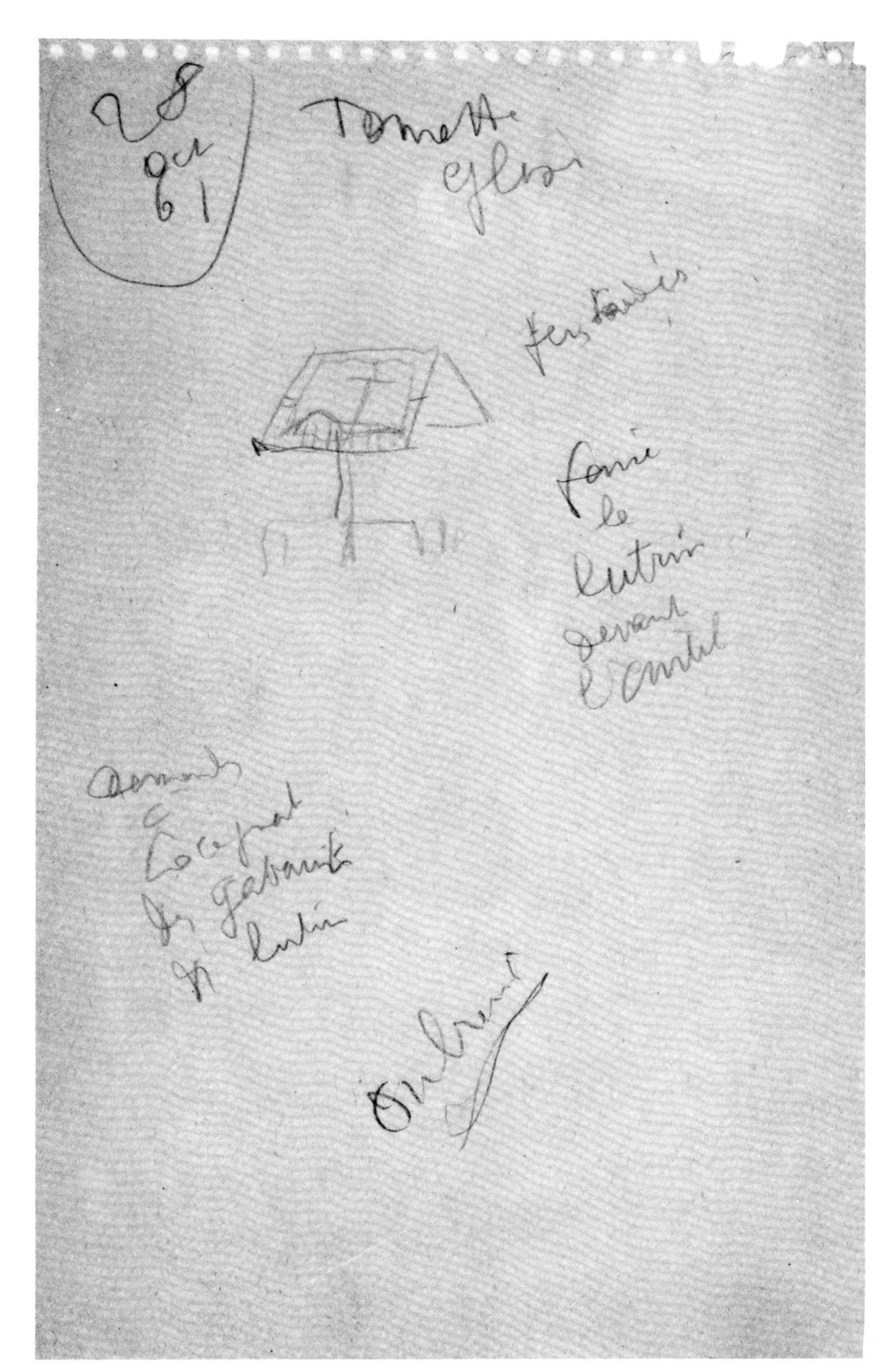

29

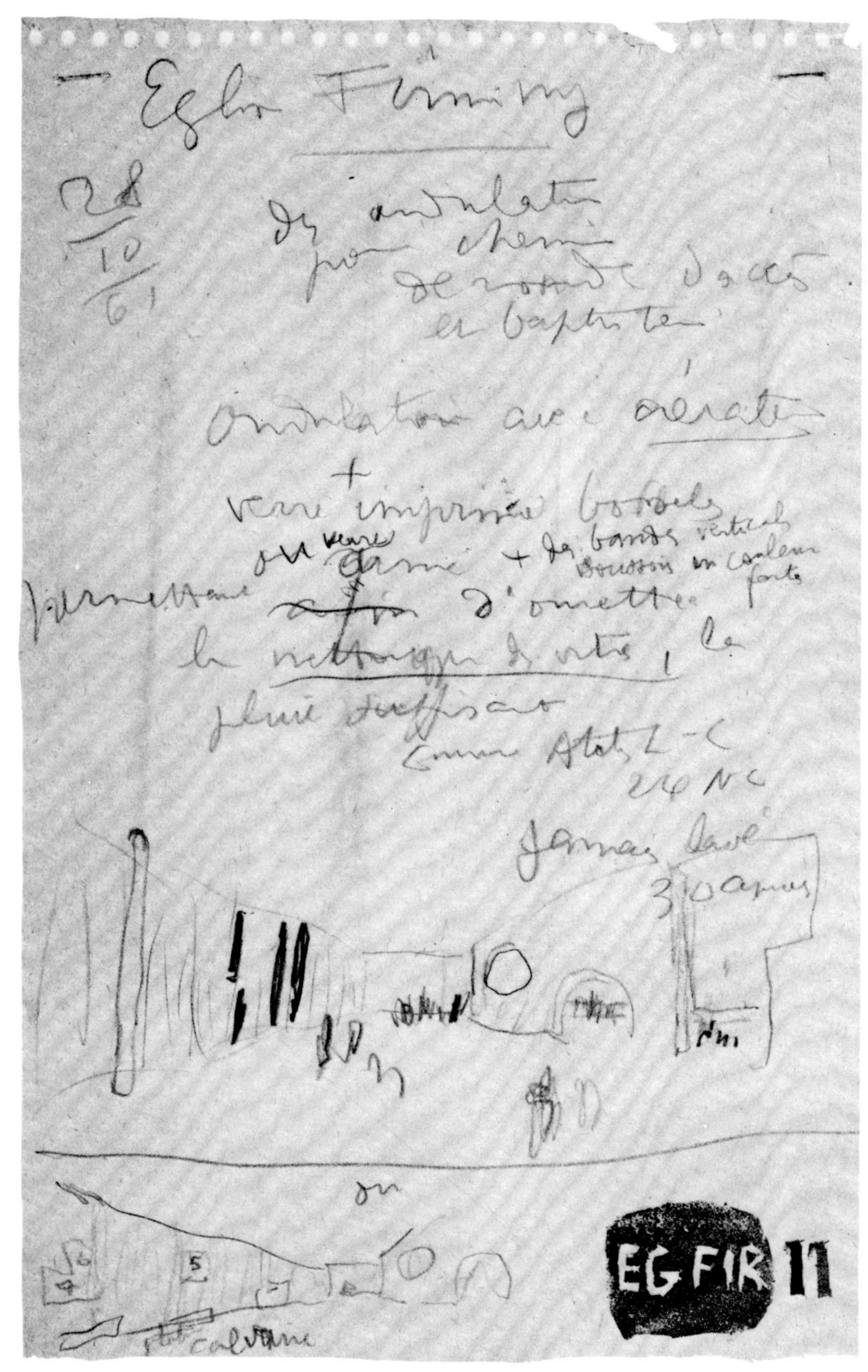

30

31 F.C., October 28, 1961.
Le Corbusier. Porch and entry study.
Notebook sketch. Pencil, paper.
5 3/8 × 11 7/8.

32 F.C., November 11, 1961, morning.
Le Corbusier. Lighting and bench
study. Ink, pencil, paper.
8 1/4 × 10 1/2.

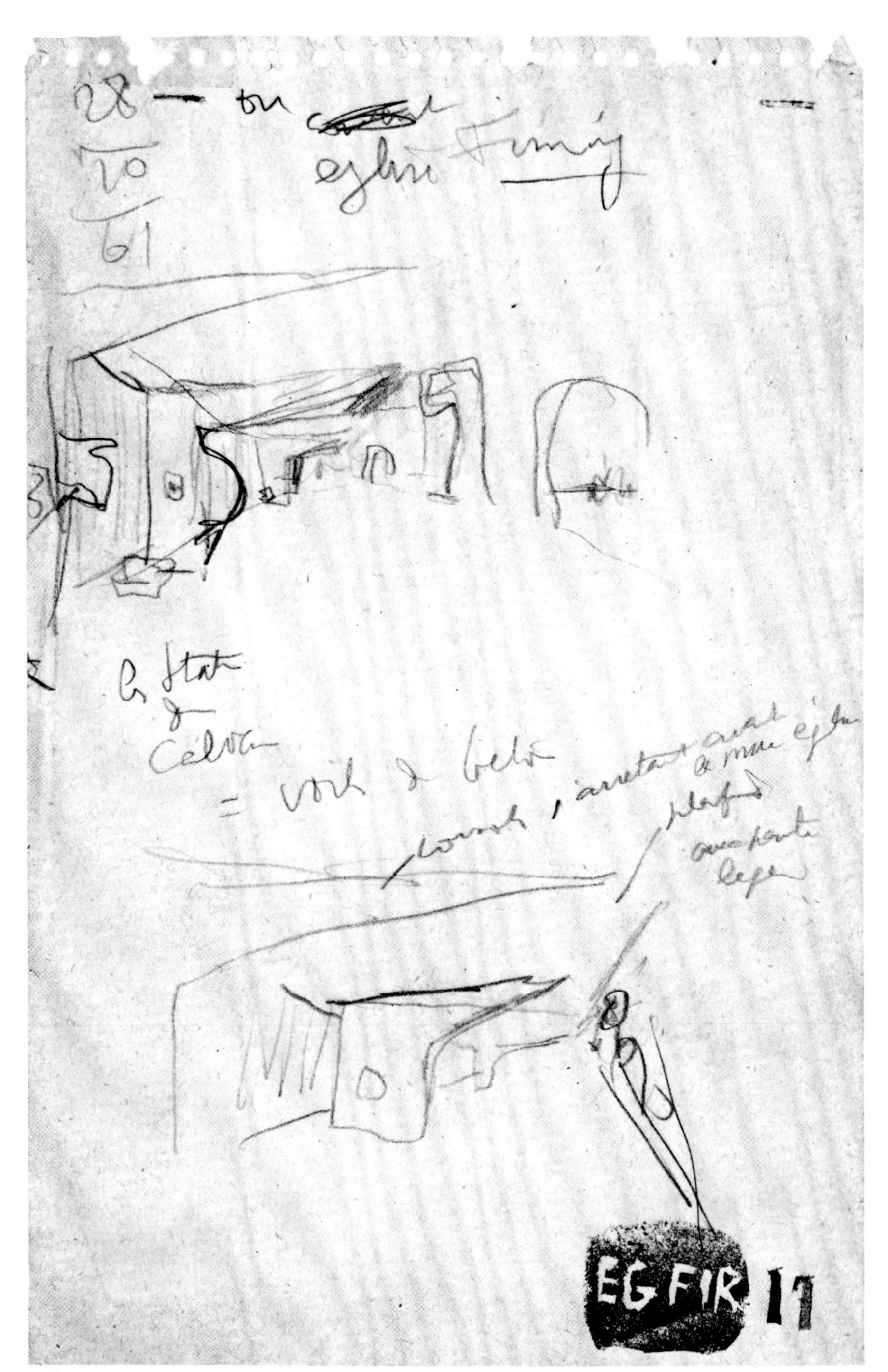

31

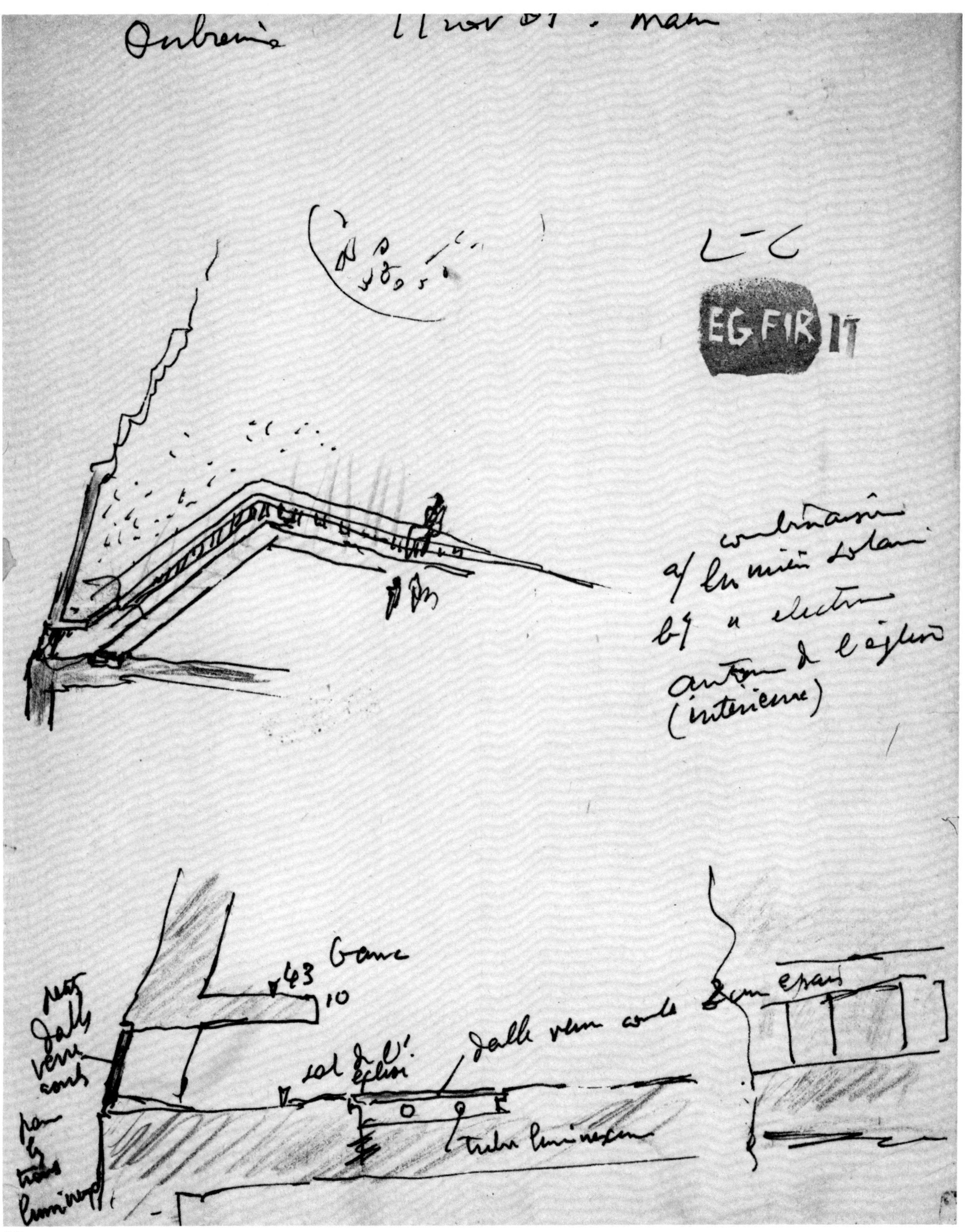
L-C
EG FIR IT
combinaison
a/ lumière solaire
b/ " électrique
autour de l'église
(intérieure)
43
10
dalle verre coulé 3cm épais
sol de l'église
tubes luminescents

43

33

34

35

33 F.C., November 1961. Jose Oubrerie in Atelier Le Corbusier. Study model: geometry.

34 F.C., November 1961. Jose Oubrerie in Atelier Le Corbusier. Study model: east and south facades.

35 F.C., November 1961. Jose Oubrerie in Atelier Le Corbusier. Study model: interior view.

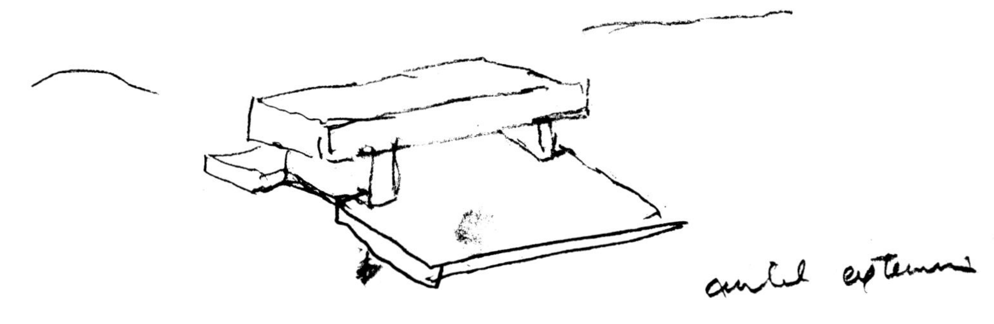

37

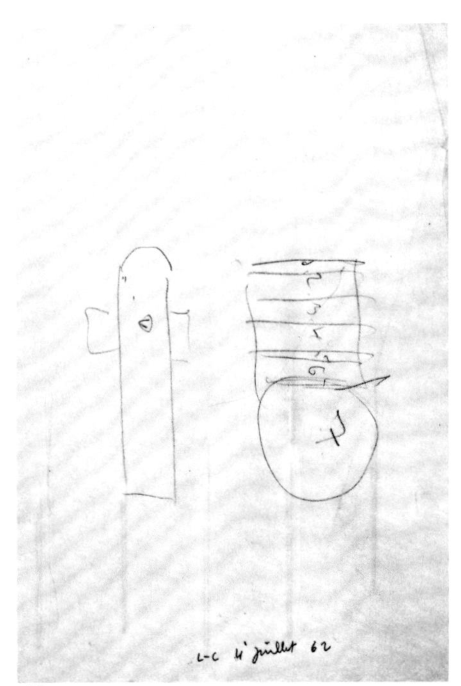

36

38

39

40

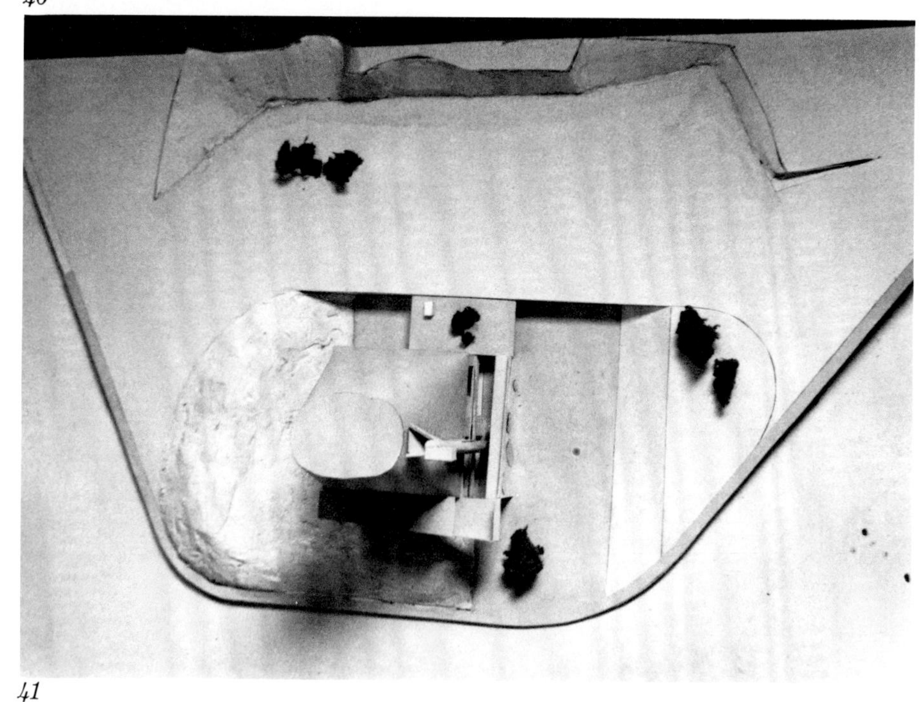

41

42

36 F.C., July 4, 1962. Le Corbusier. Variable container and variable contents: incrementation of people between weekdays and Sundays. Pencil, paper. 8 1/4×10 1/2.

37 F.C., January 8, 1962. Le Corbusier. External altar study of the Chapel of Ronchamp, detail. Pencil, paper. 8 1/4×10 1/2.

38 F.C., February 1962. Jose Oubrerie in Atelier Le Corbusier. Model, first stage view of west and south facades.

39 F.C., March 1962. Le Corbusier. Site study. Pencil, paper. 15 1/2×23.

40 F.C., March 1962. Jose Oubrerie in Atelier Le Corbusier. Model, third level. Cardboard.

41 F.C., February 1962. Jose Oubrerie in Atelier Le Corbusier. Model, first stage view from plane.

42 F.C., March 1962. Le Corbusier. Notes on structure. Pencil, paper. 8 1/4×10 1/2.

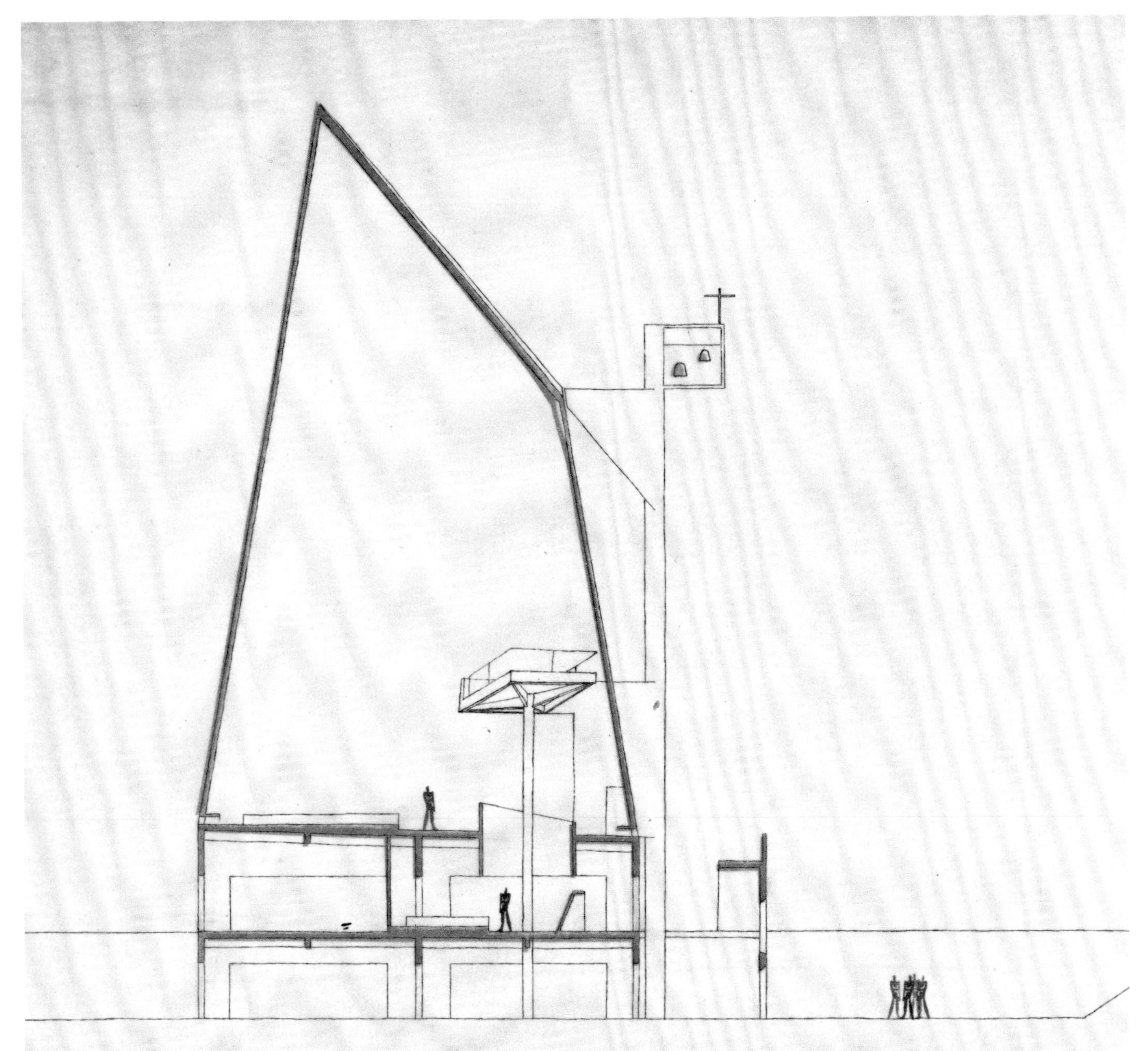

43

43 F.C., June 25, 1962. Jose Oubrerie in Atelier Le Corbusier. North/south section. 27 3/8×21.

44 F.C., June 25, 1962. Jose Oubrerie in Atelier Le Corbusier. East/West section. Ink, draft paper, zipatone. 27 3/8×21. (Sec. no. 6005.)

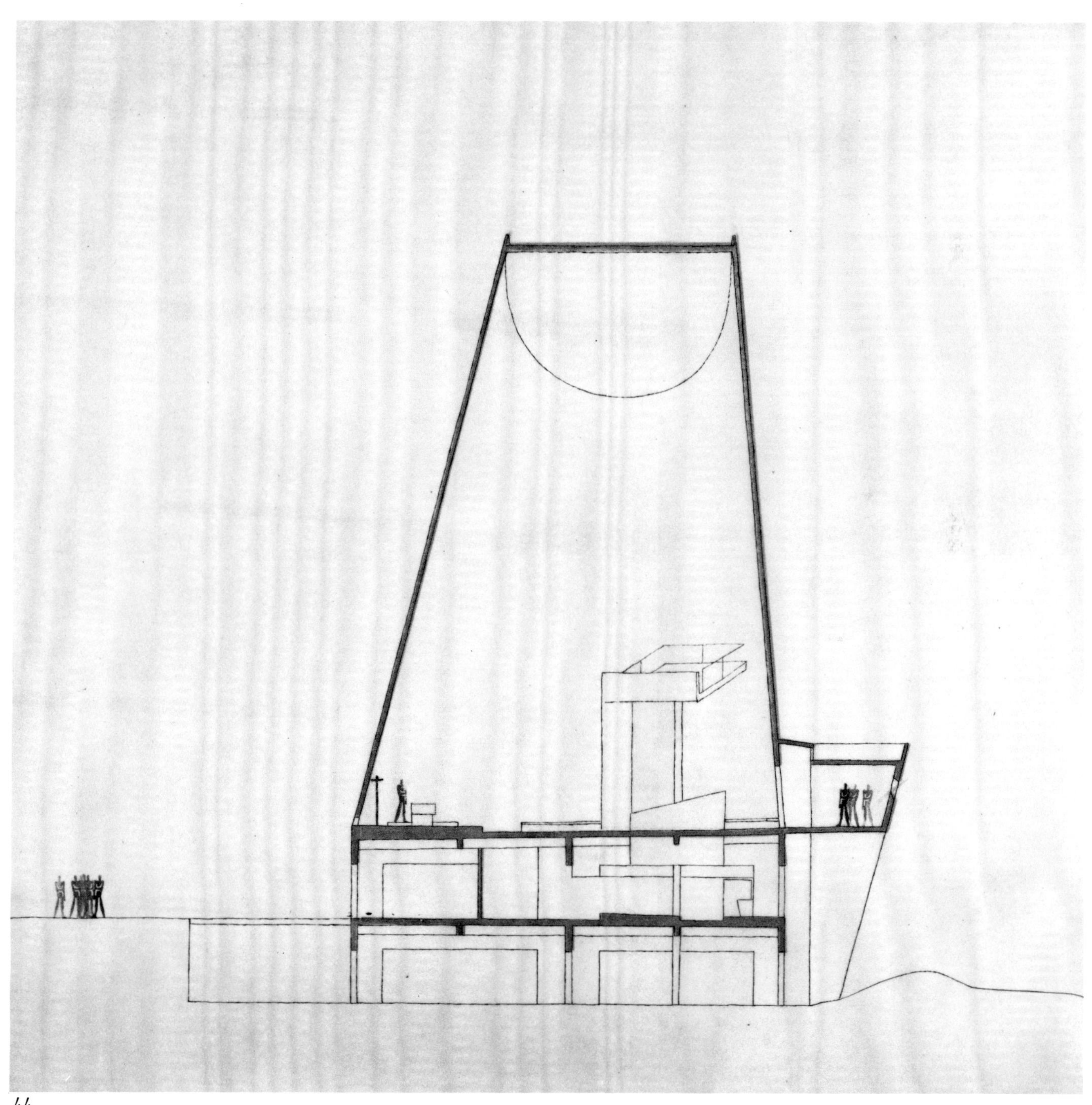

44

45

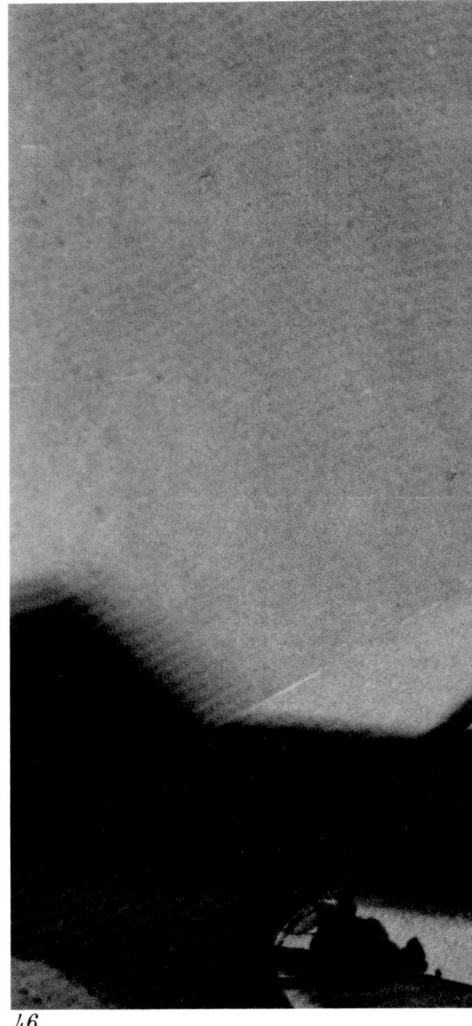

46

45 F.C., October 1962. Le Corbusier. West elevation. Colored pencil, print. 26 1/8 × 20 15/16.

46 F.C., October 1962. Jose Oubrerie in Atelier Le Corbusier (signed by Le Corbusier). Model, view from above. Tempera, cardboard. 28 × 21.

52

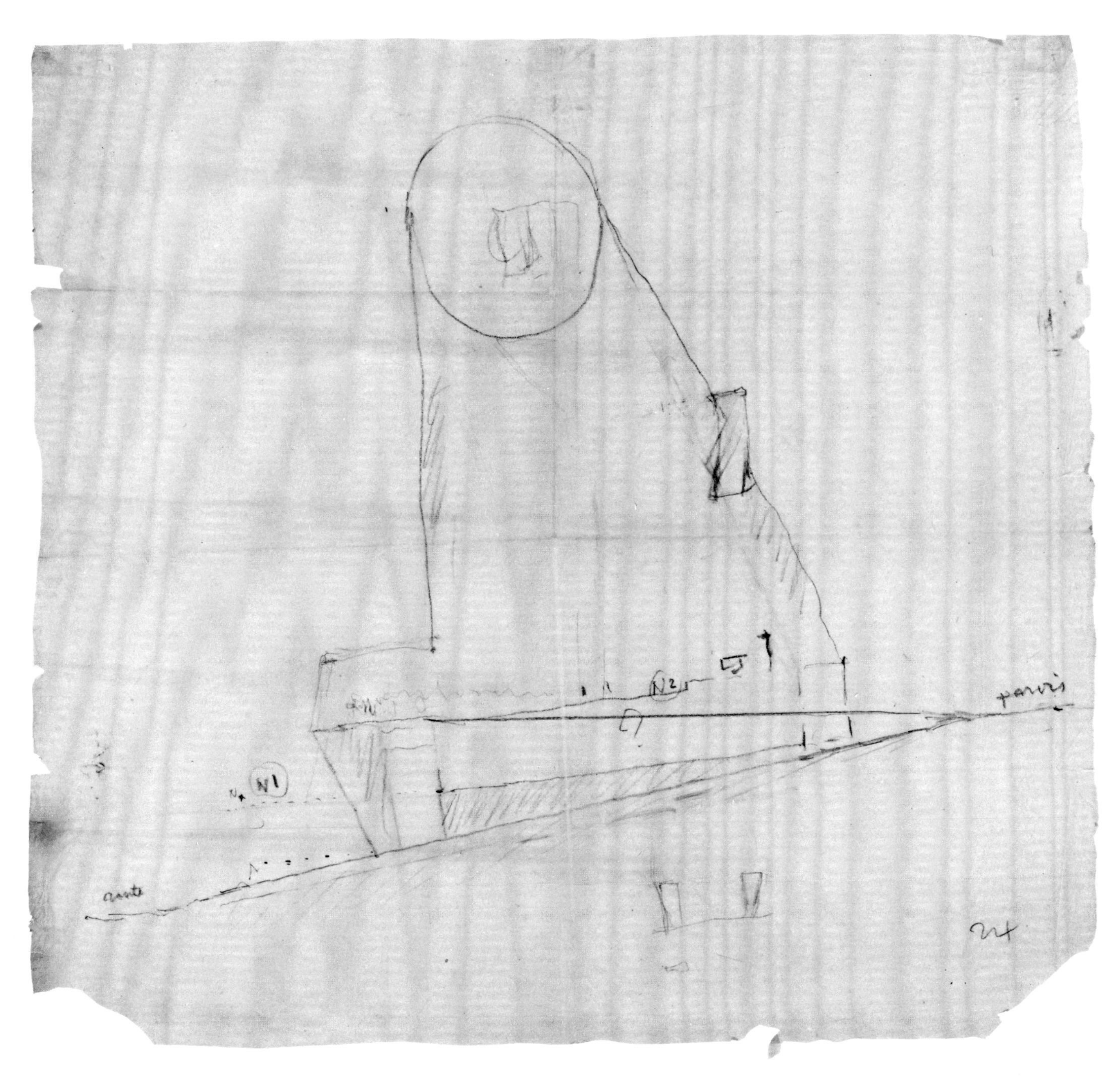

47 F.C., November 1962.
Le Corbusier. Sketch showing certain enforced economies: the reduction in the cone height and the realignment of the entry from the ground. Colored pencil, draft paper. 24 1/4 20 1/8.

48 F.C., October 1962. Jose Oubrerie in Atelier Le Corbusier. Model, south facade.

49 F.C., October 1962. Jose Oubrerie in Atelier Le Corbusier. Model, west facade.

50 F.C., October 1962. Jose Oubrerie in Atelier Le Corbusier. Model, east facade.

48

49

50

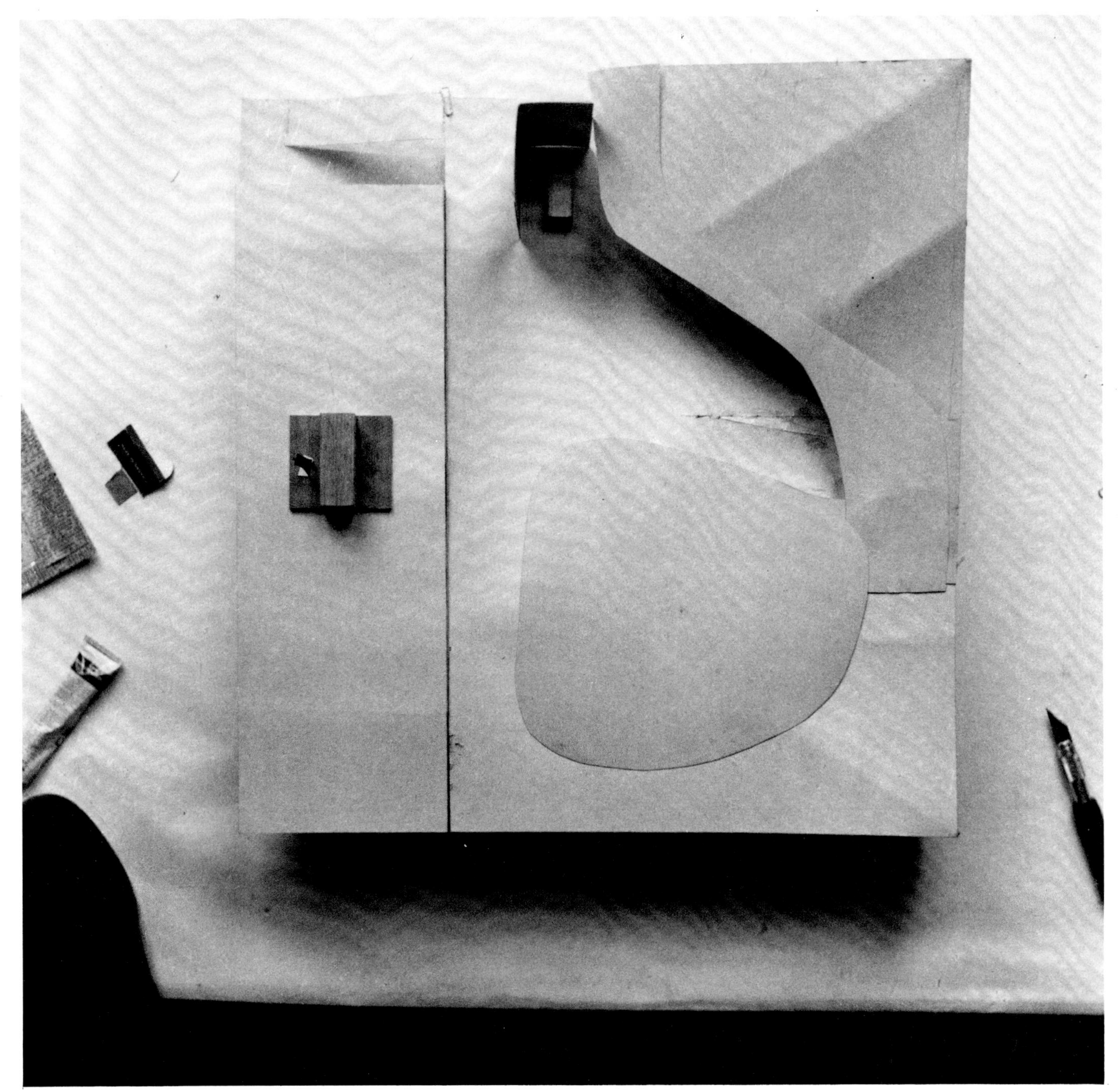

51

51, 53 F.C., November 28, 1962. Jose Oubrerie in Atelier Le Corbusier. Study model: Chapel and Church, fourth and fifth levels; introduction of spiral floor.

52 F.C., November 1962. Jose Oubrerie in Atelier Le Corbusier. Church floor study. (F.LC. Sec. no. 16561.)

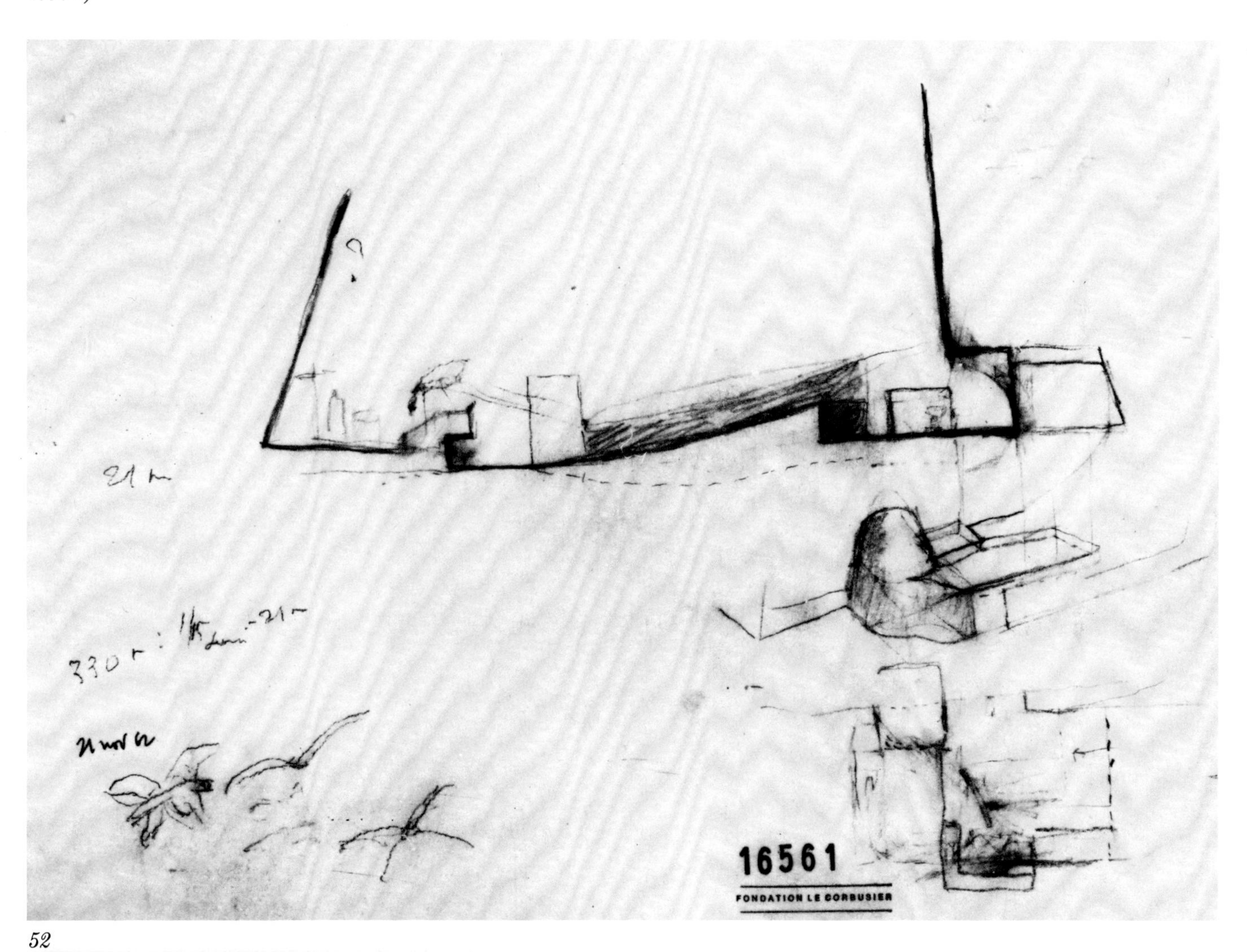

52

53

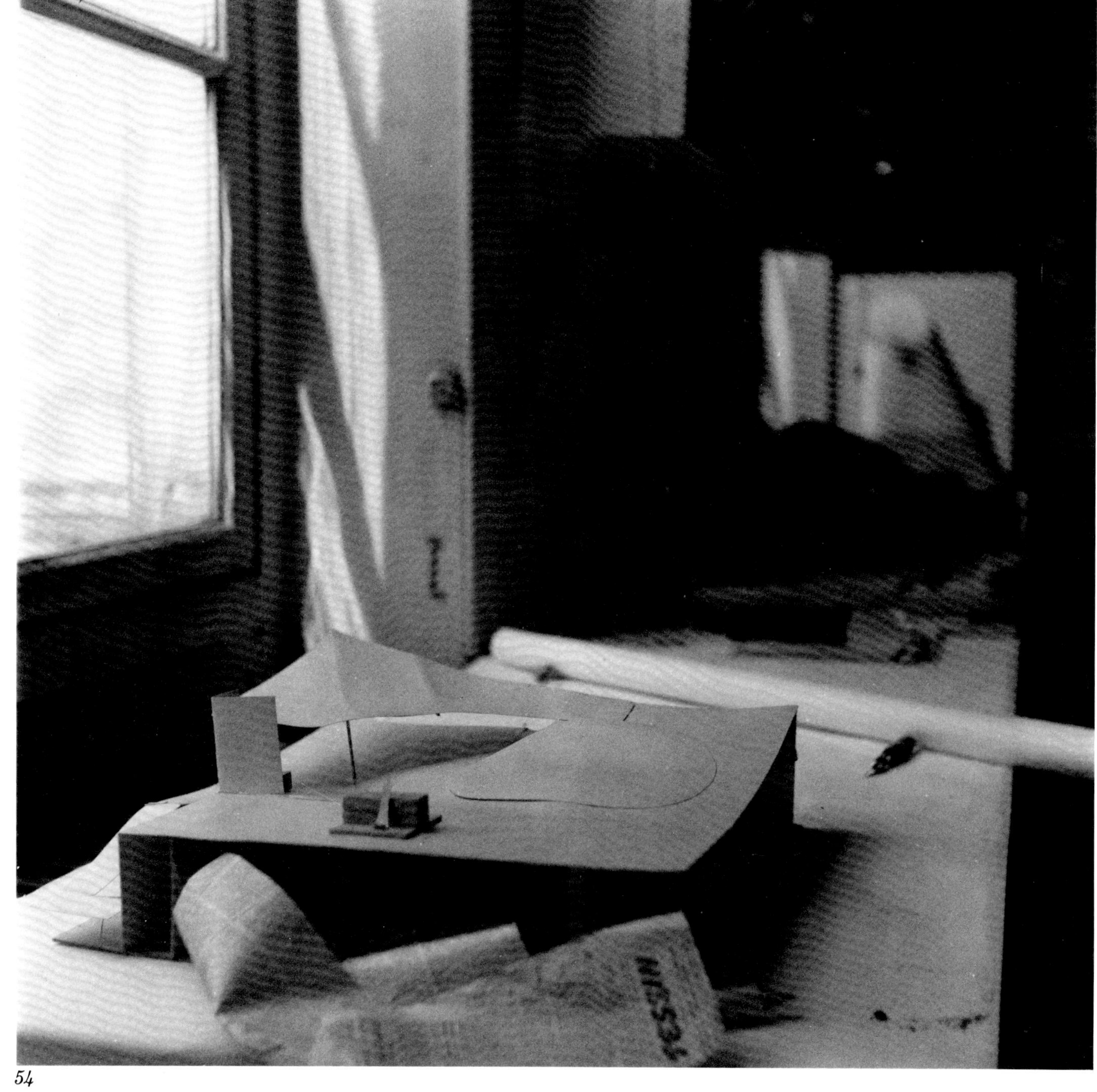

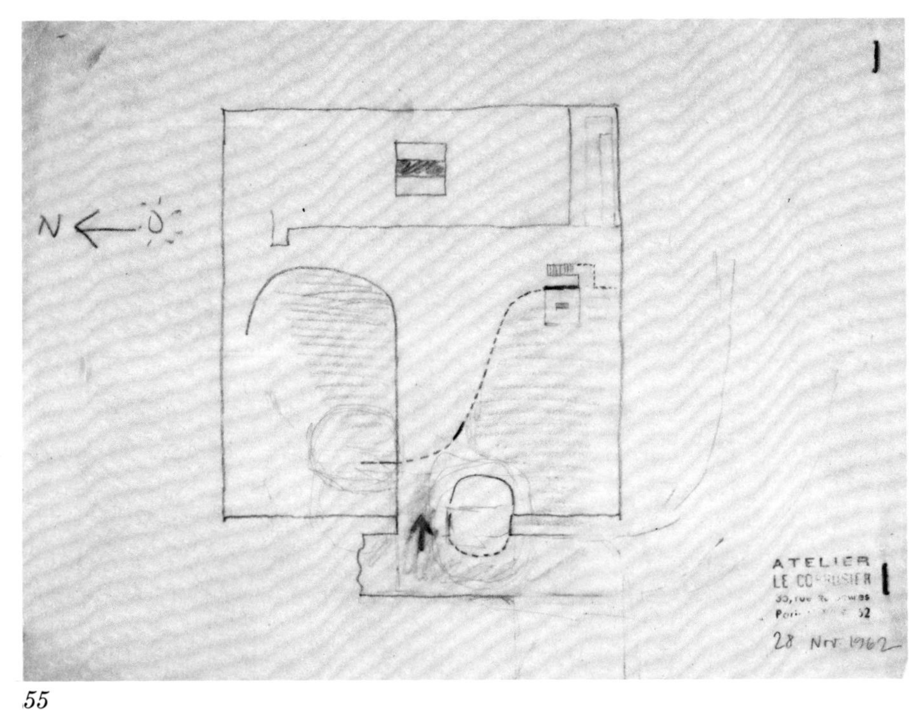

55

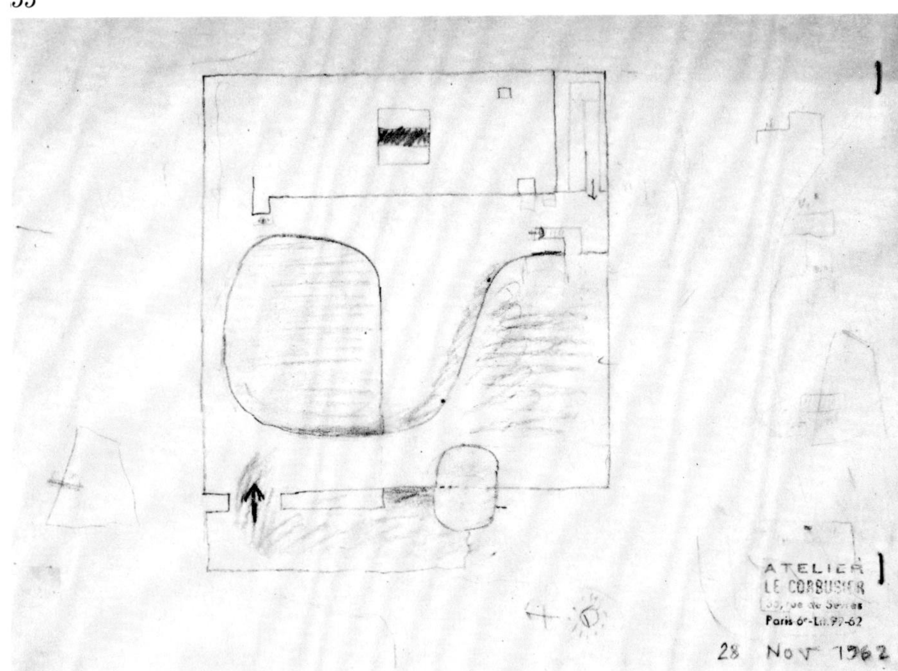

56

54 F.C., November 28, 1962. Jose Oubrerie in Atelier Le Corbusier. Study model: Chapel and Church, fourth and fifth levels; introduction of spiral floor.

55 F.C., November 28, 1962. Jose Oubrerie in Atelier Le Corbusier. Fourth level plan; conclusive drawing. Colored pencil, paper. 10 5/8×8 1/4.

56 F.C., November 1962. Jose Oubrerie in Atelier Le Corbusier. Fifth level plan; conclusive drawing.

57

57 F.C., November 28, 1962. Jose Oubrerie in Atelier Le Corbusier. Study model: west facade, shell.

58 F.C., November 1962. Le Corbusier. Pre-site-visit study (references to Gisors and the Templars). Colored pencil, paper. 20 5/8 × 14 3/4.

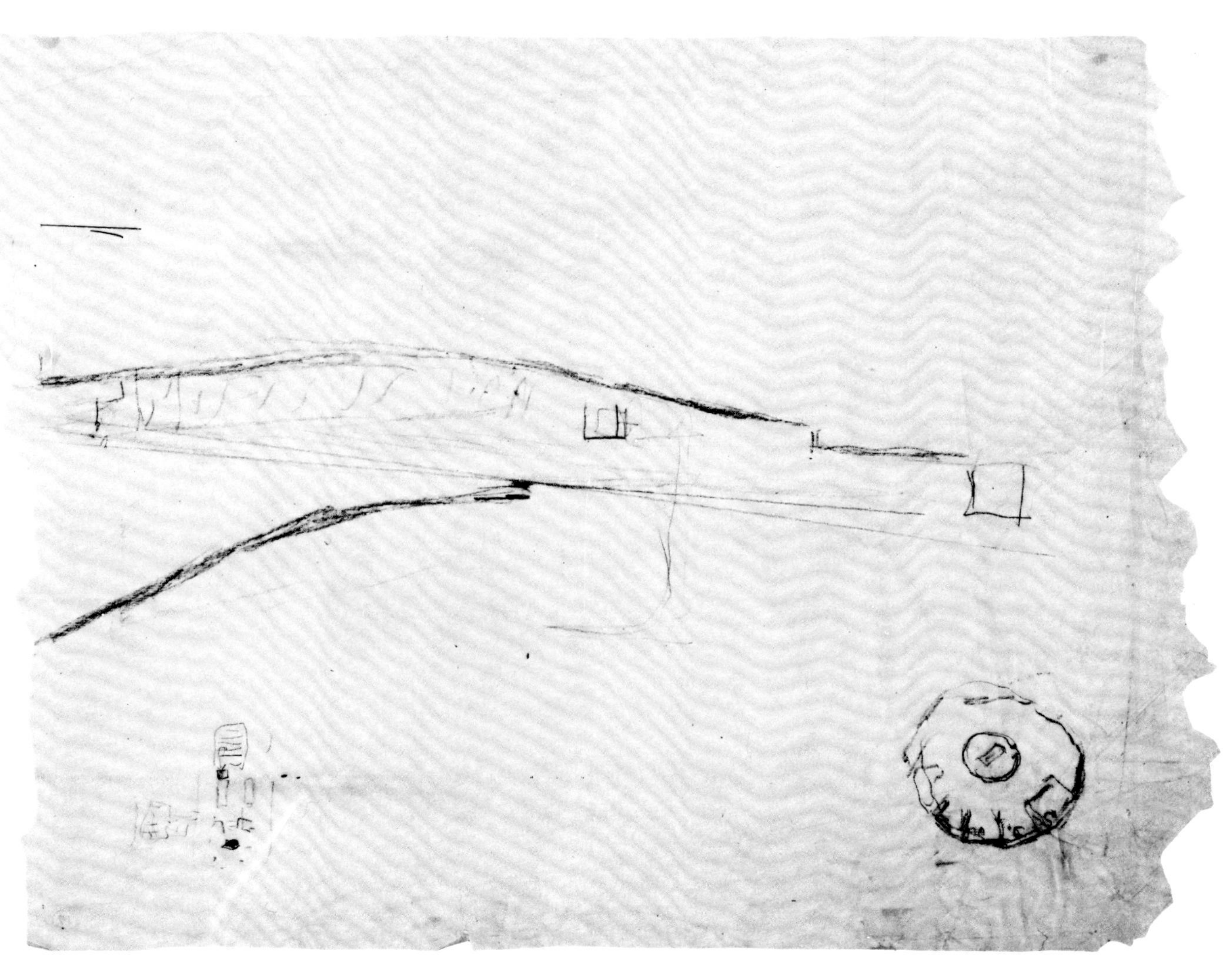

58

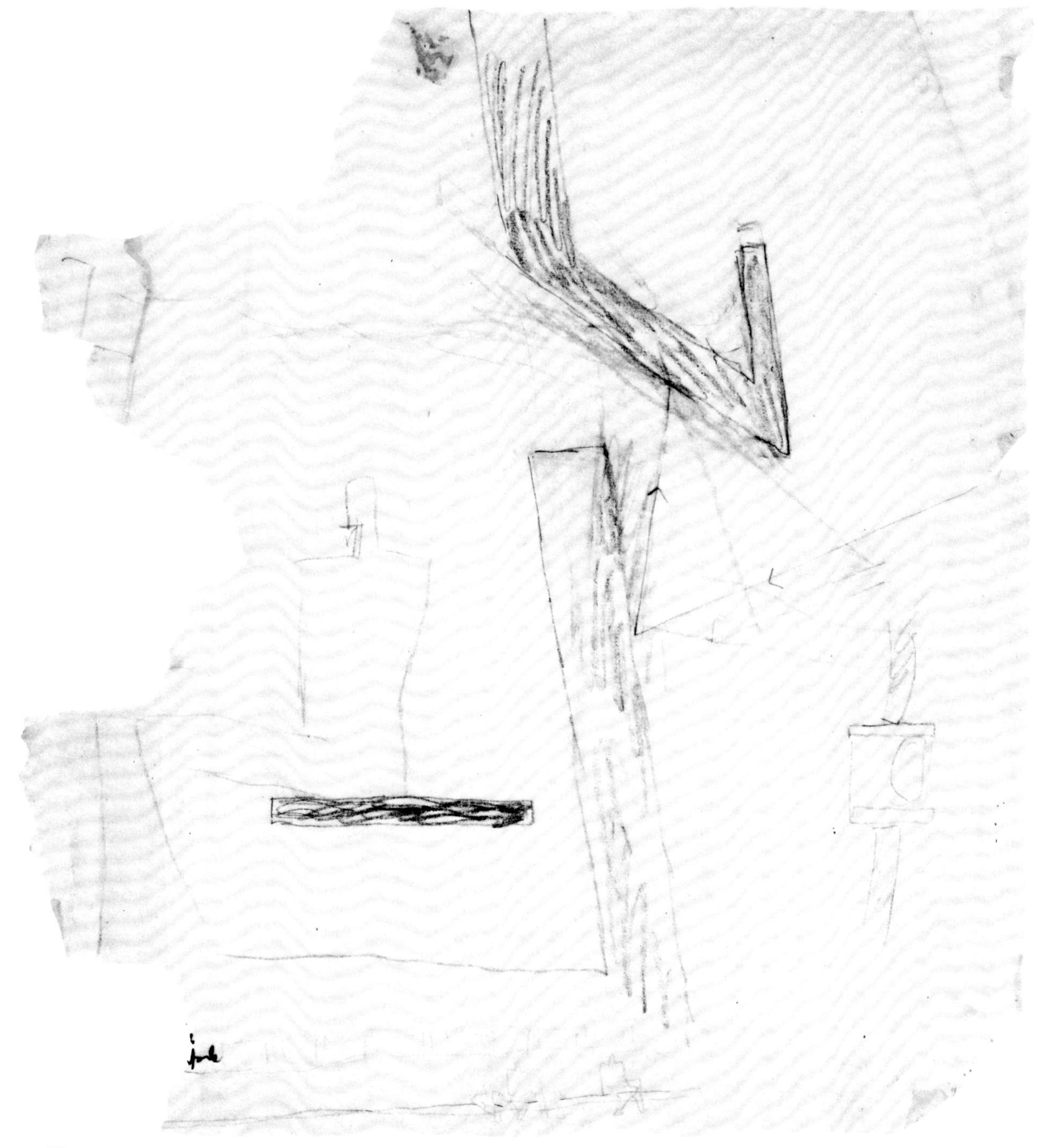

59

59 F.C., November 11, 1962. Le Corbusier and Jose Oubrerie. Horizontal gutter window study. Colored pencil, paper. 11×11 3/16.

60 F.C., November 1962. Le Corbusier. Drawing indicating the surrounding horizontal light (gutter window) following the shape of the floors. Pencil, paper. 8 1/4×10 1/2.

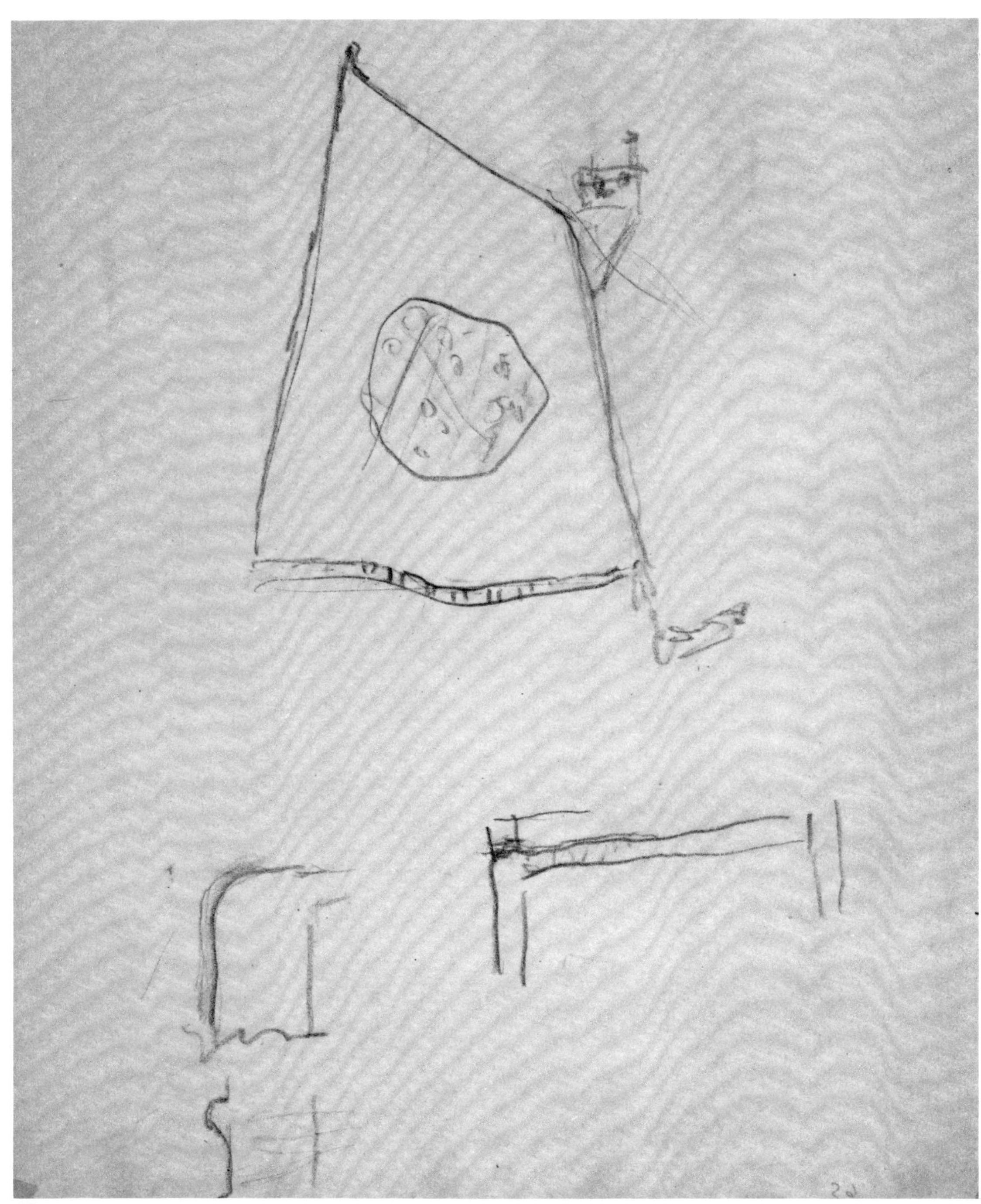

60

61 *F.C., December 19, 1962. Le Corbusier. Seasonal light study. Colored pencil, paper. 16 7/8×11 3/16.*

62 *F.C., December 19, 1962. Le Corbusier. Drawing showing parallel between Assembly building cone in Chandigarh and Firminy Church. Pencil, paper. 8 1/4×10 1/2.*

63 *F.C., December 20, 1962. Le Corbusier. Acoustic study; casting inside the shell. Pencil, paper. 8 1/4×10 1/2.*

62

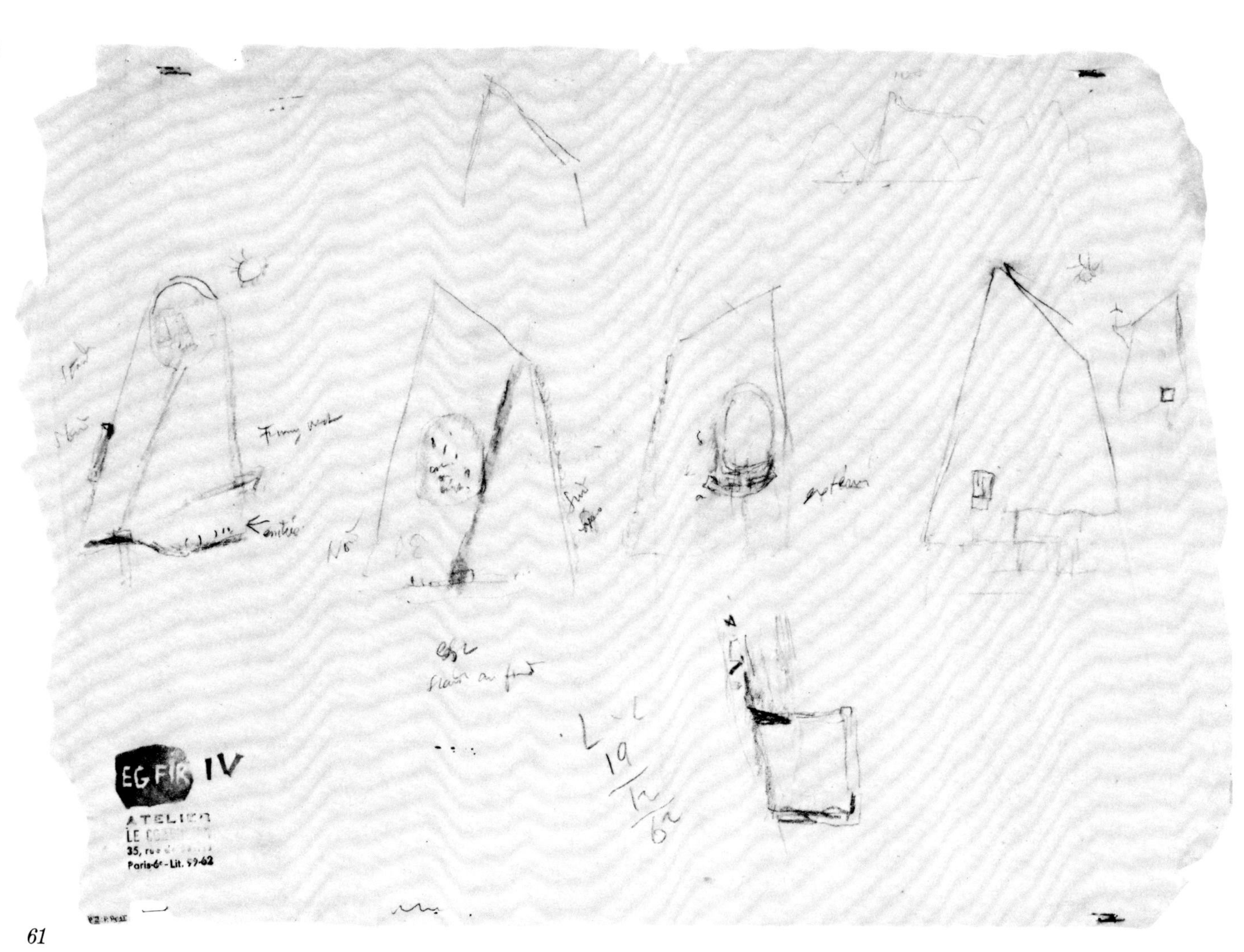

61

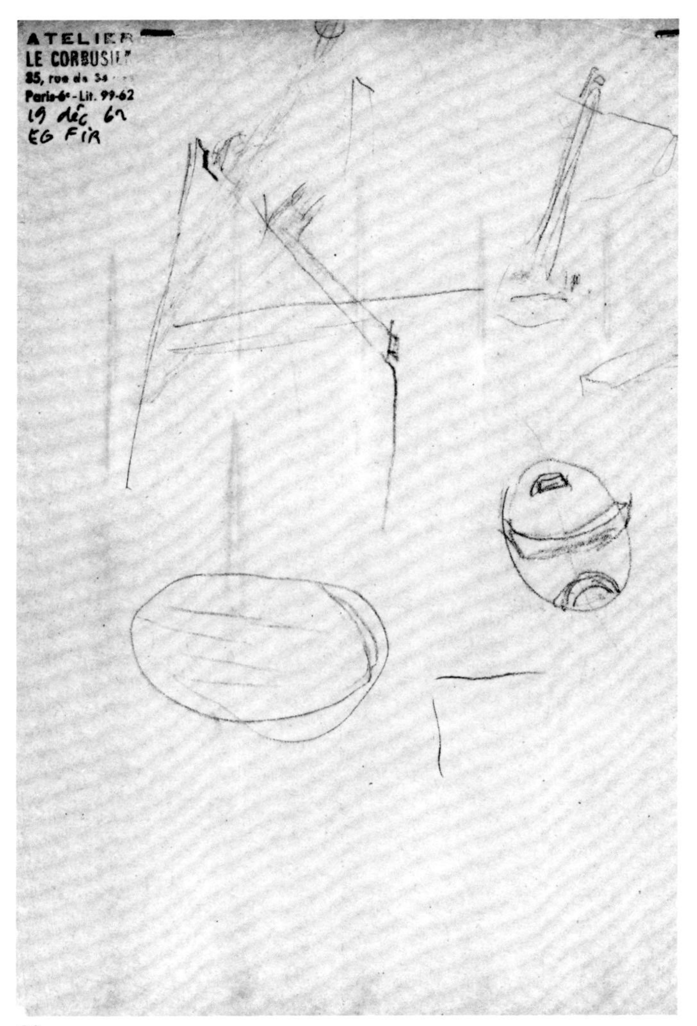
ATELIER
LE CORBUSIER
Paris-6e - Lit. 99-62
19 déc 62
EG FIR

62

63

EG FIR
ATELIER
LE CORBUSIER
35, rue de Sèvres
Paris-6e - Lit. 99-62
20 déc 62

64 *64 F.C., December 1962. Jose Oubrerie in Atelier Le Corbusier. Street facing the Church. Pencil, paper. 9 13/16×9 7/8.*

65 F.C., December 30, 1962. Le Corbusier. Site study. Pencil, paper. 14 7/8×14 1/2.

66, 67, 68 F.C., December 1962. Le Corbusier. Bell tower and gutter study. Pencil, paper. 8 1/4×10 1/2.

69 F.C., December 1962. Le Corbusier. Light, bell tower and gutter study. Pencil, paper. 8 1/4×10 1/2.

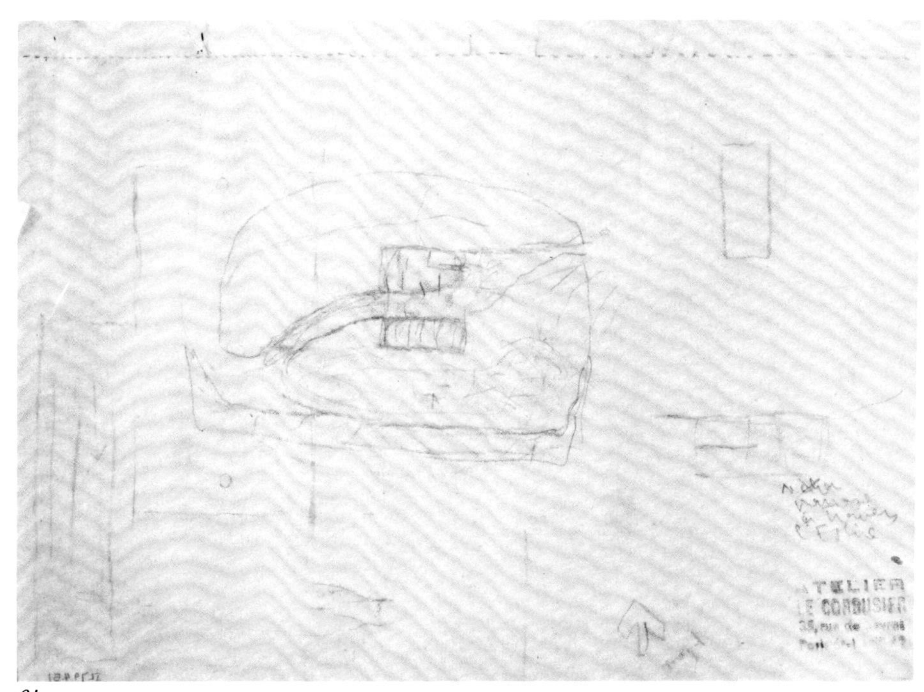

64

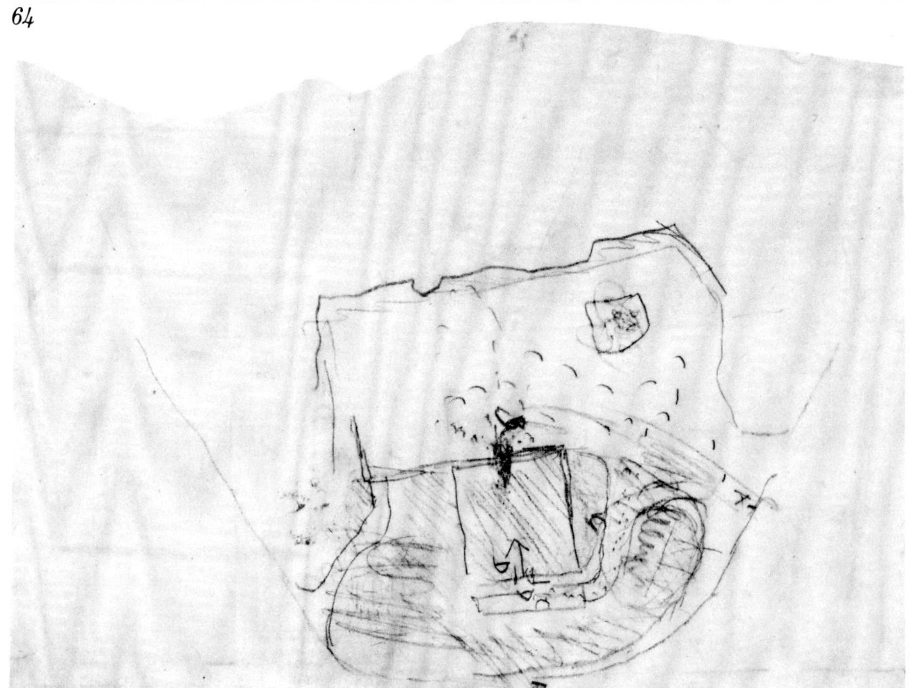

65

ATELIER
LE CORBUSIER
1 L-C

66

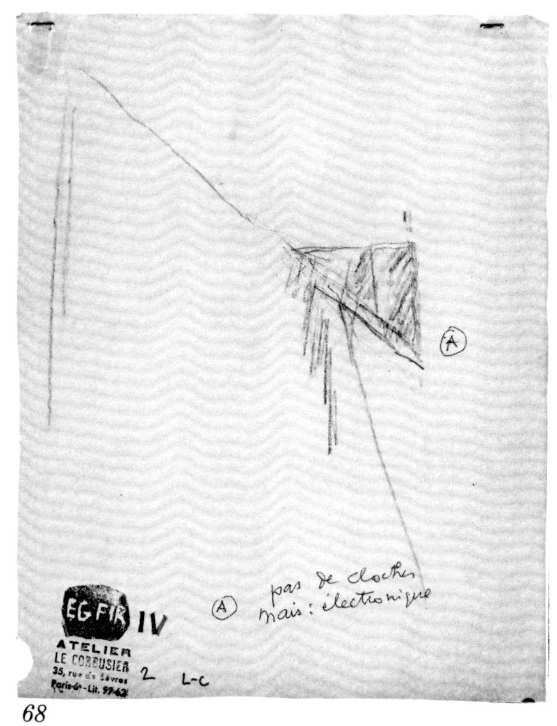
Ⓐ
EGFIR IV
Ⓐ pas de cloches
mais: électronique
ATELIER
LE CORBUSIER
35, rue de Sèvres
2 L-C

68

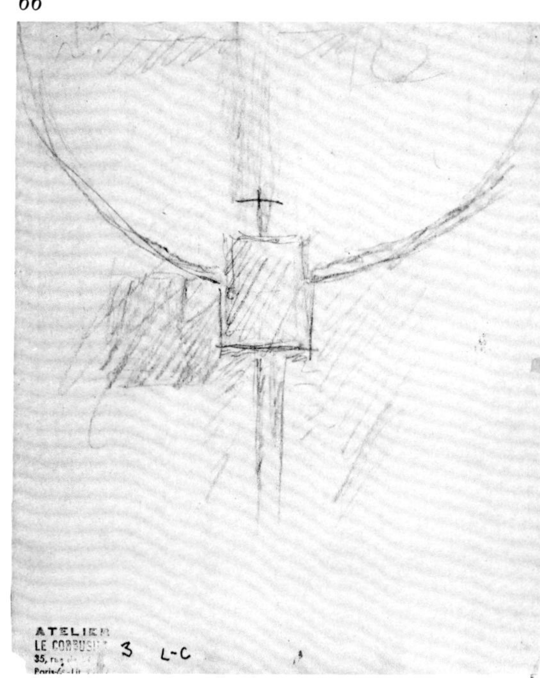
ATELIER
3 L-C

67

ATELIER
4 L-C

69

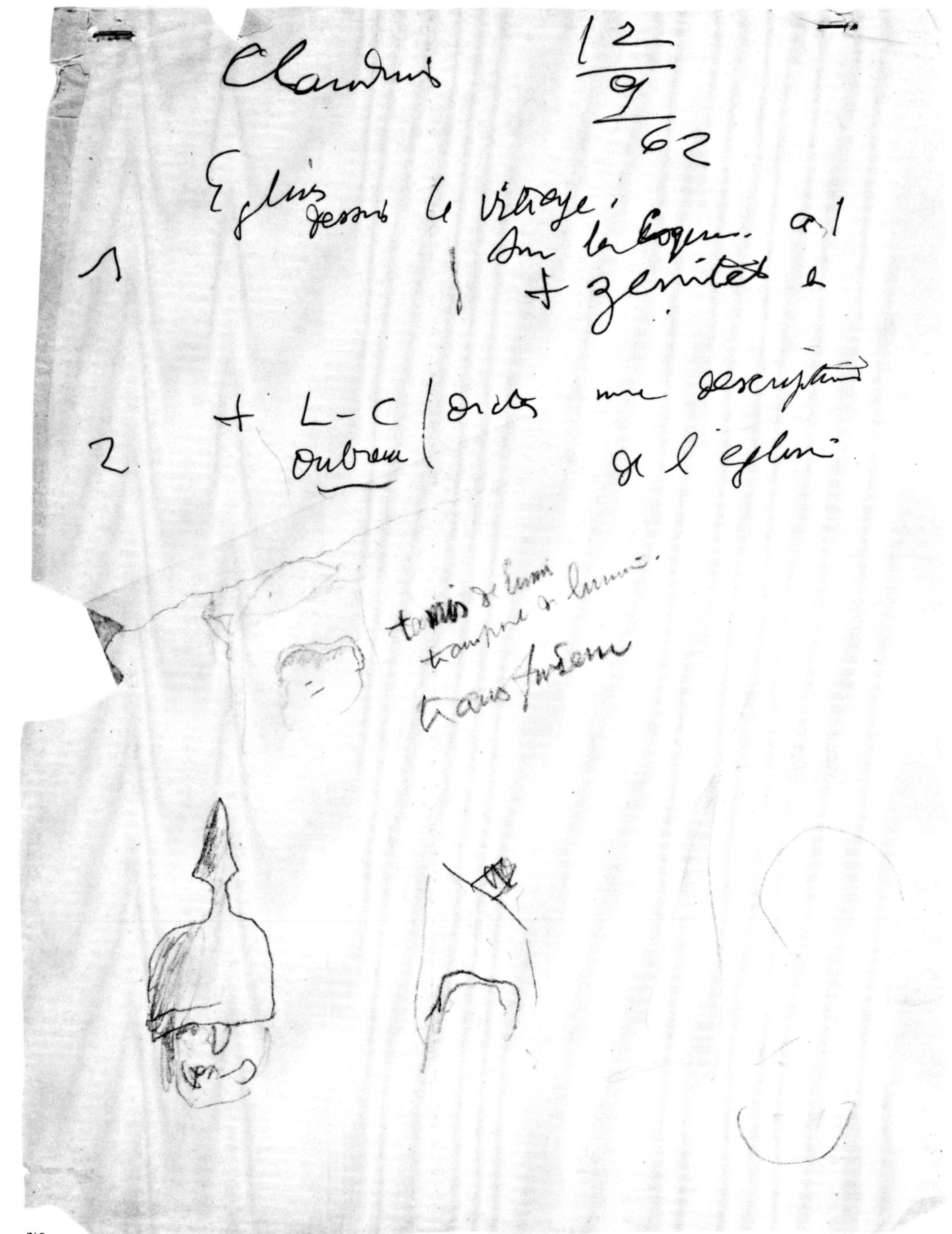

70

70 F.C., September 13, 1962. Le Corbusier. Comparison between a World War I German Helmet and the profile of the church: necessity of the top elements. Ink, pencil, paper. 8 1/4×10 1/2.

71 F.C., June 25, 1962. Jose Oubrerie in Atelier Le Corbusier. First level plan, classrooms and main meeting room. Ink, draft paper, zipatone. 27 3/8×21. (Pl. no. 6001.)

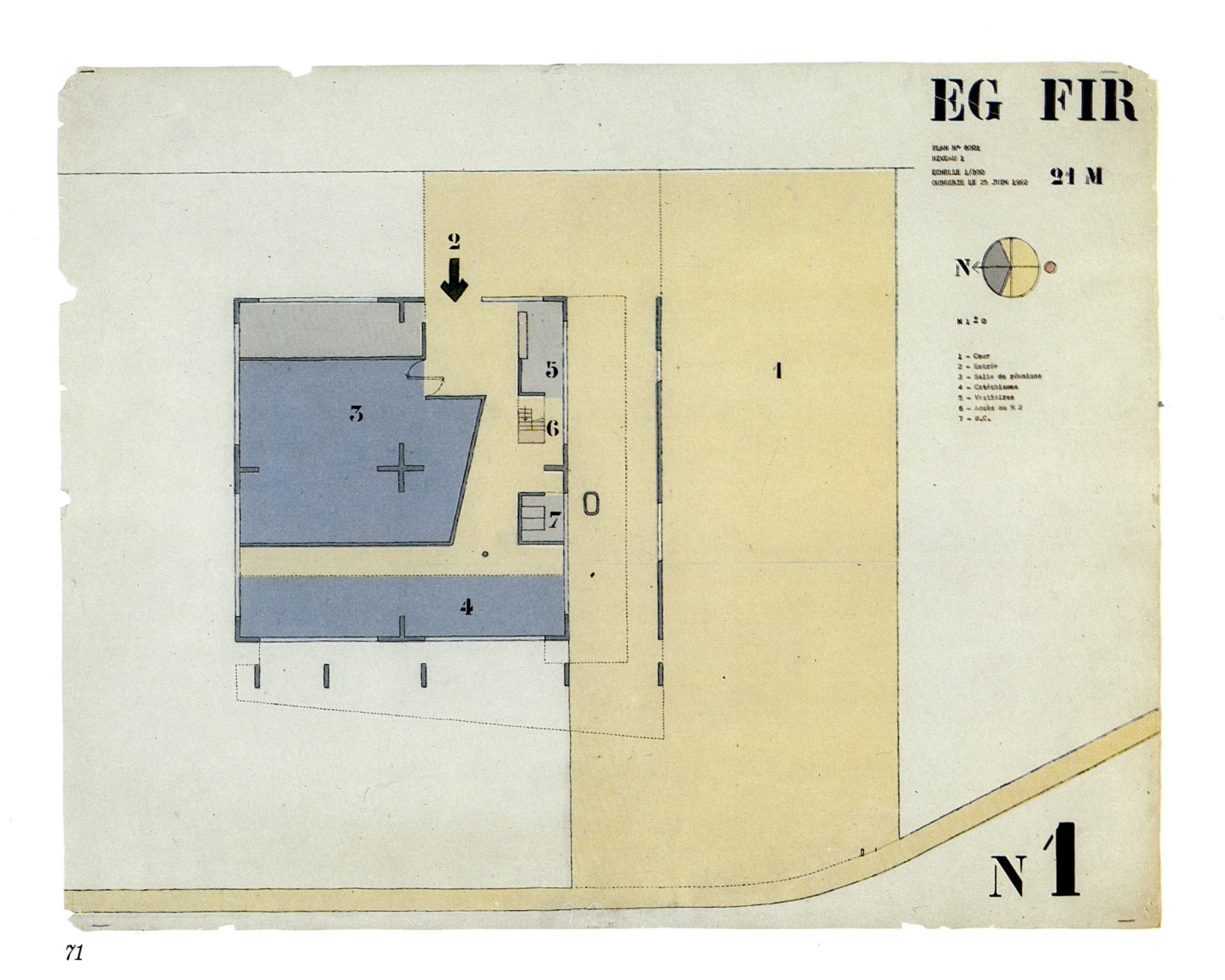

71

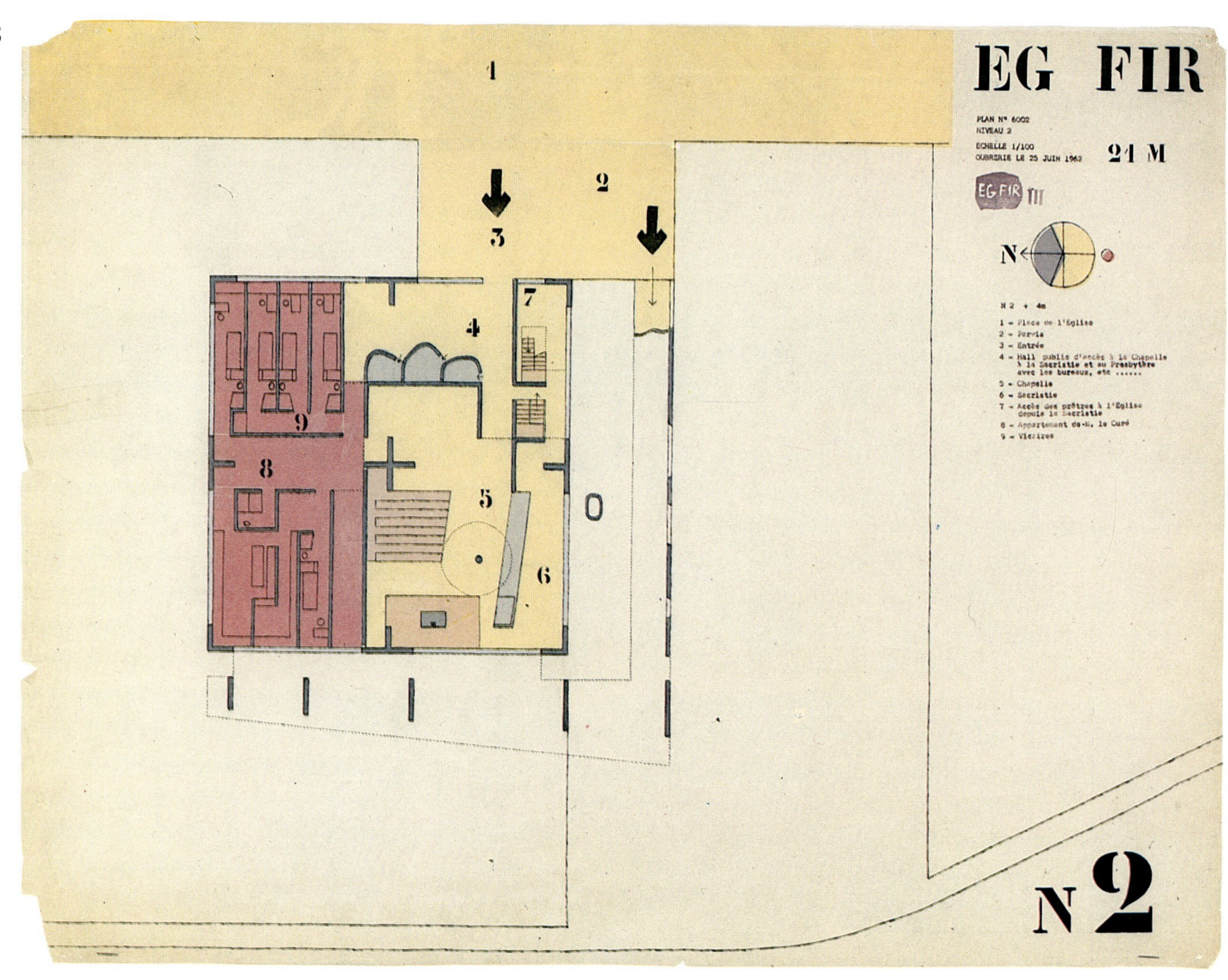
EG FIR
PLAN N° 6002
NIVEAU 2
ECHELLE 1/100
OUBRERIE LE 25 JUIN 1962
24 M
EG FIR
N
N 2 + 4m
1 - Place de l'Eglise
2 - Parvis
3 - Entrée
4 - Hall public d'accès à la Chapelle à la Sacristie et au Presbytère avec les bureaux, etc ......
5 - Chapelle
6 - Sacristie
7 - Accès des prêtres à l'Eglise depuis la Sacristie
8 - Appartement de M. le Curé
9 - Vicaires
1
2
3
4
5
6
7
8
9
N 2

72

72 F.C., June 25, 1962. Jose Oubrerie in Atelier Le Corbusier. Second level plan, piazza entrance hall, sacristy and parish house. Ink, draft paper, zipatone. 27 3/8 × 21. (Pl. no. 6002.)

73 F.C., June 25, 1962. Jose Oubrerie in Atelier Le Corbusier. Third level plan, ramp and Church entrance. Ink, draft paper, zipatone. 27 3/8 × 21.(Pl. no. 6003.)

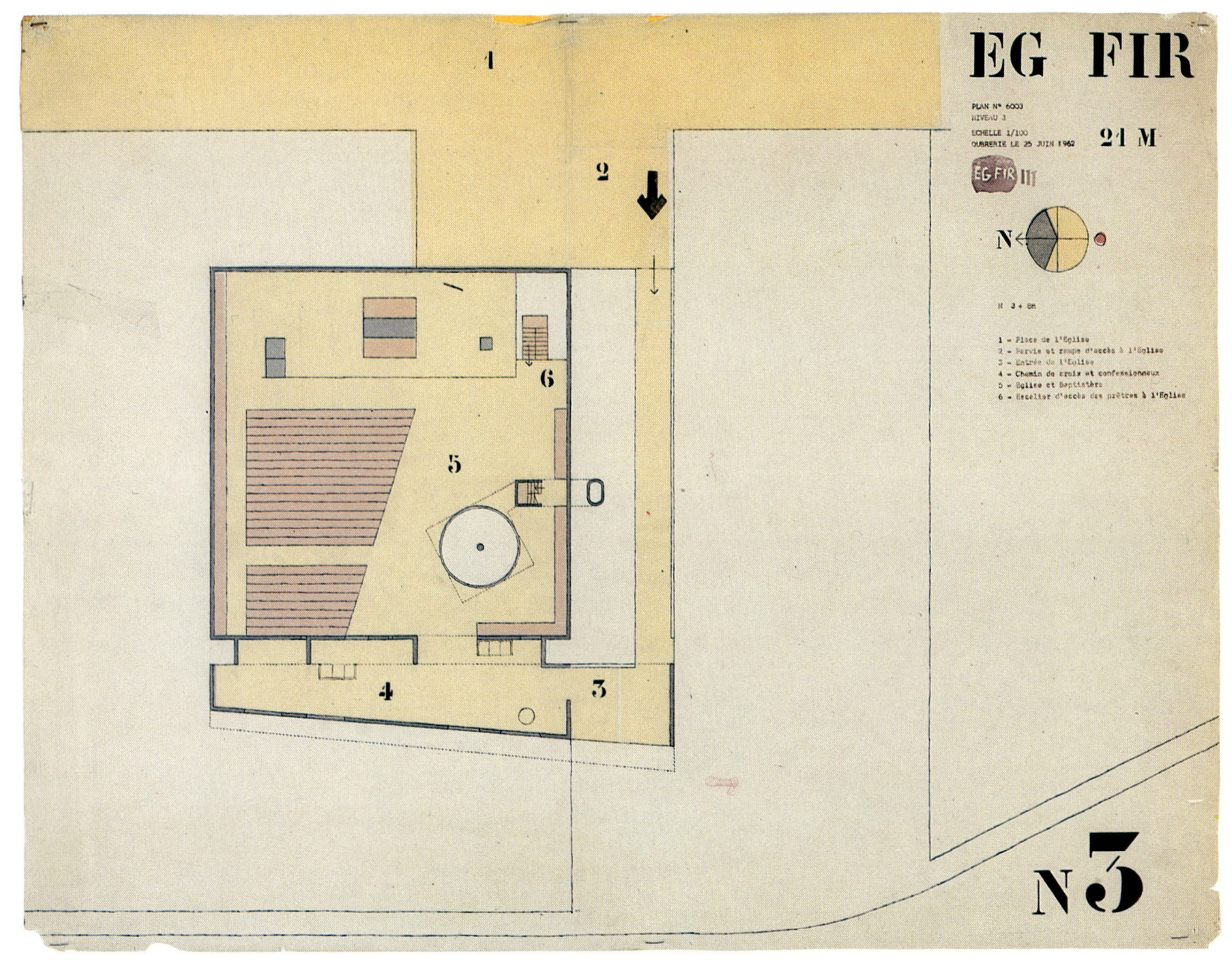

73

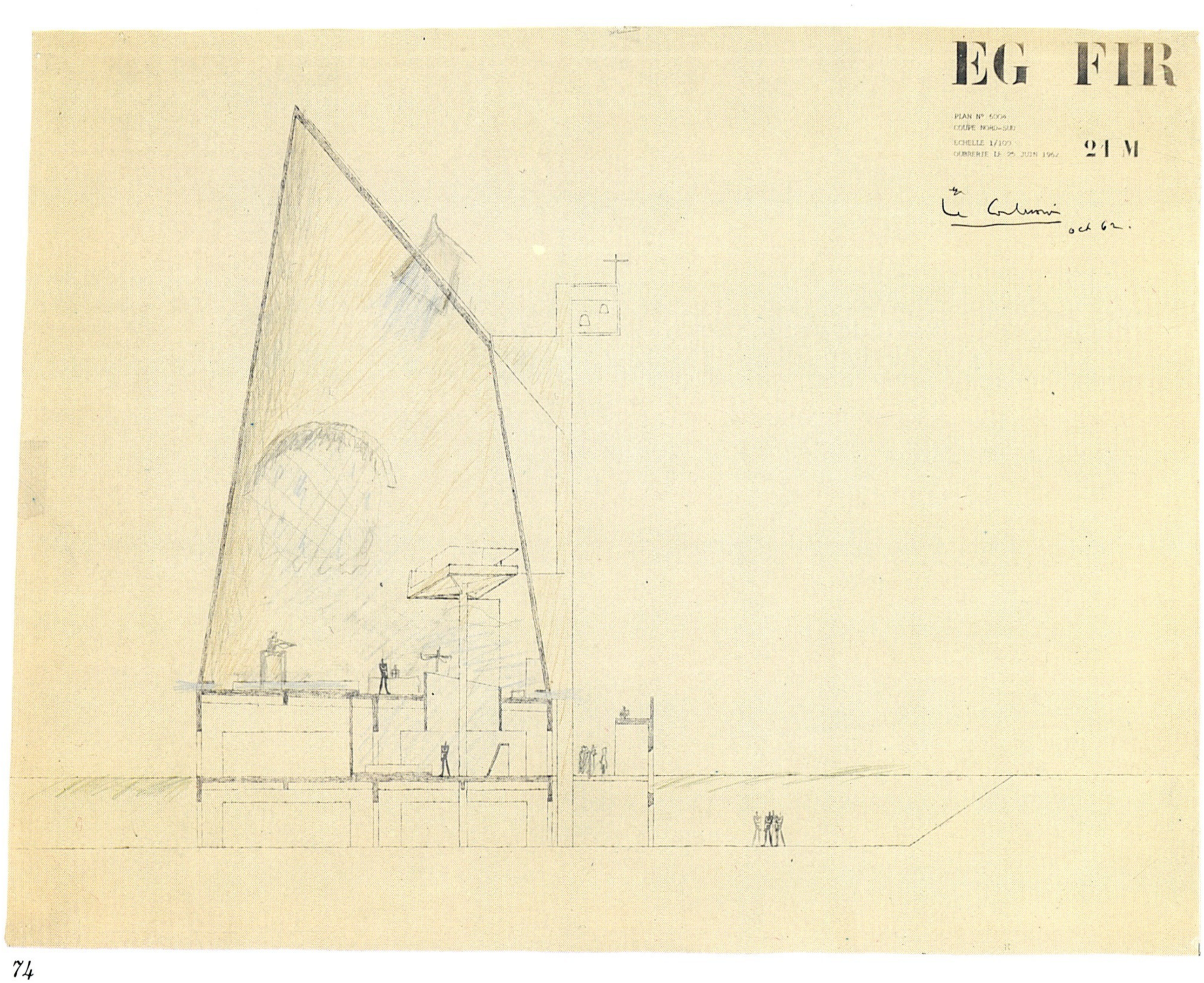

74

74 F.C., October 1962. Le Corbusier. West/east section. Colored pencil, print. 27 3/4 × 20 5/8.

75 F.C., October 1962. Le Corbusier. East elevation. Colored pencil, print. 26 1/8 × 20 15/16.

75

72

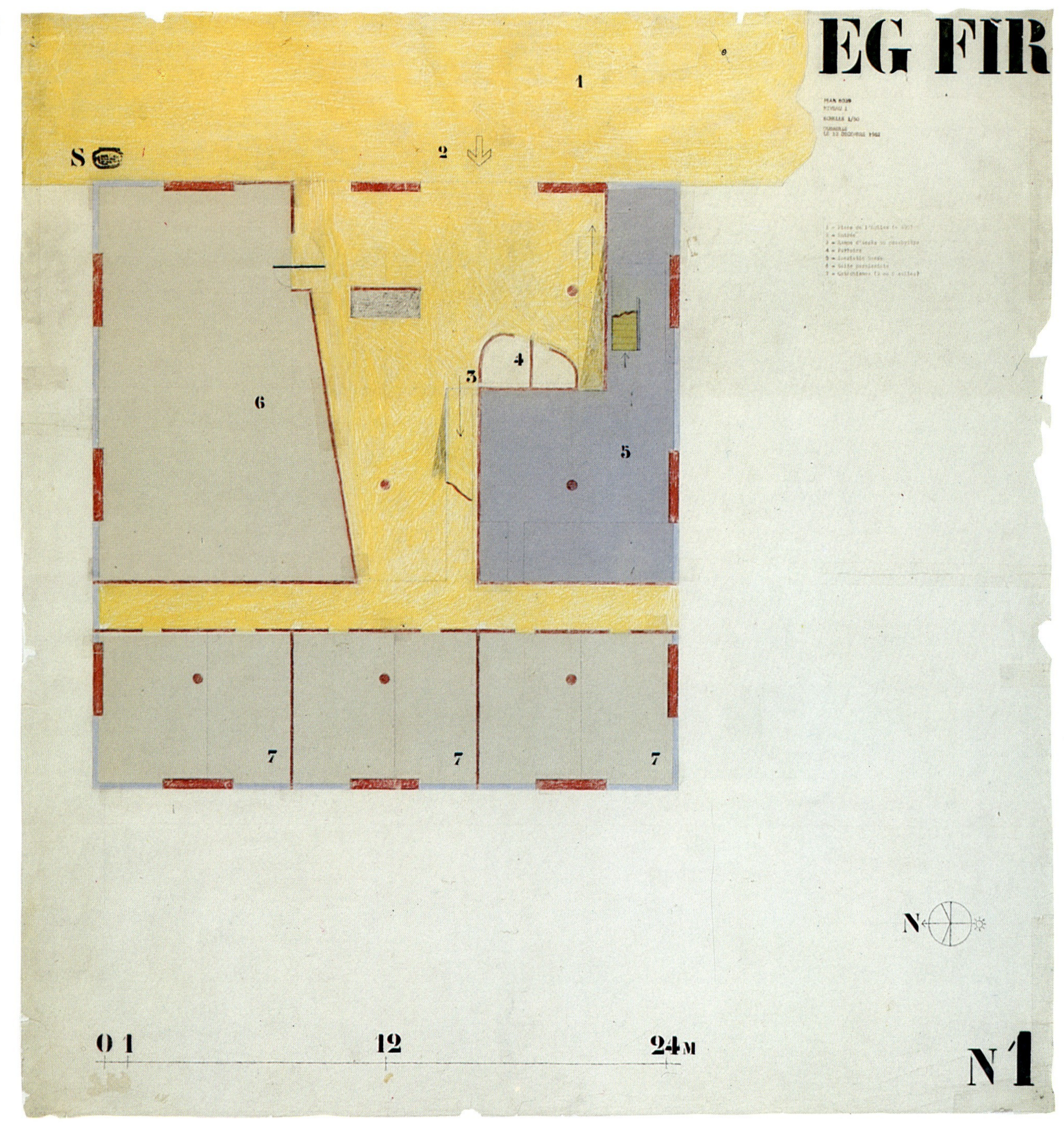

76 F.C., December 12, 1962. Jose Oubrerie in Atelier Le Corbusier. First level plan. Pencil, paper. 35×36. (Pl. no. 6039.)

77 F.C., December 12, 1962. Jose Oubrerie in Atelier Le Corbusier. Second level plan. Pencil, paper. 35×36. (Pl. nl. 6040.)

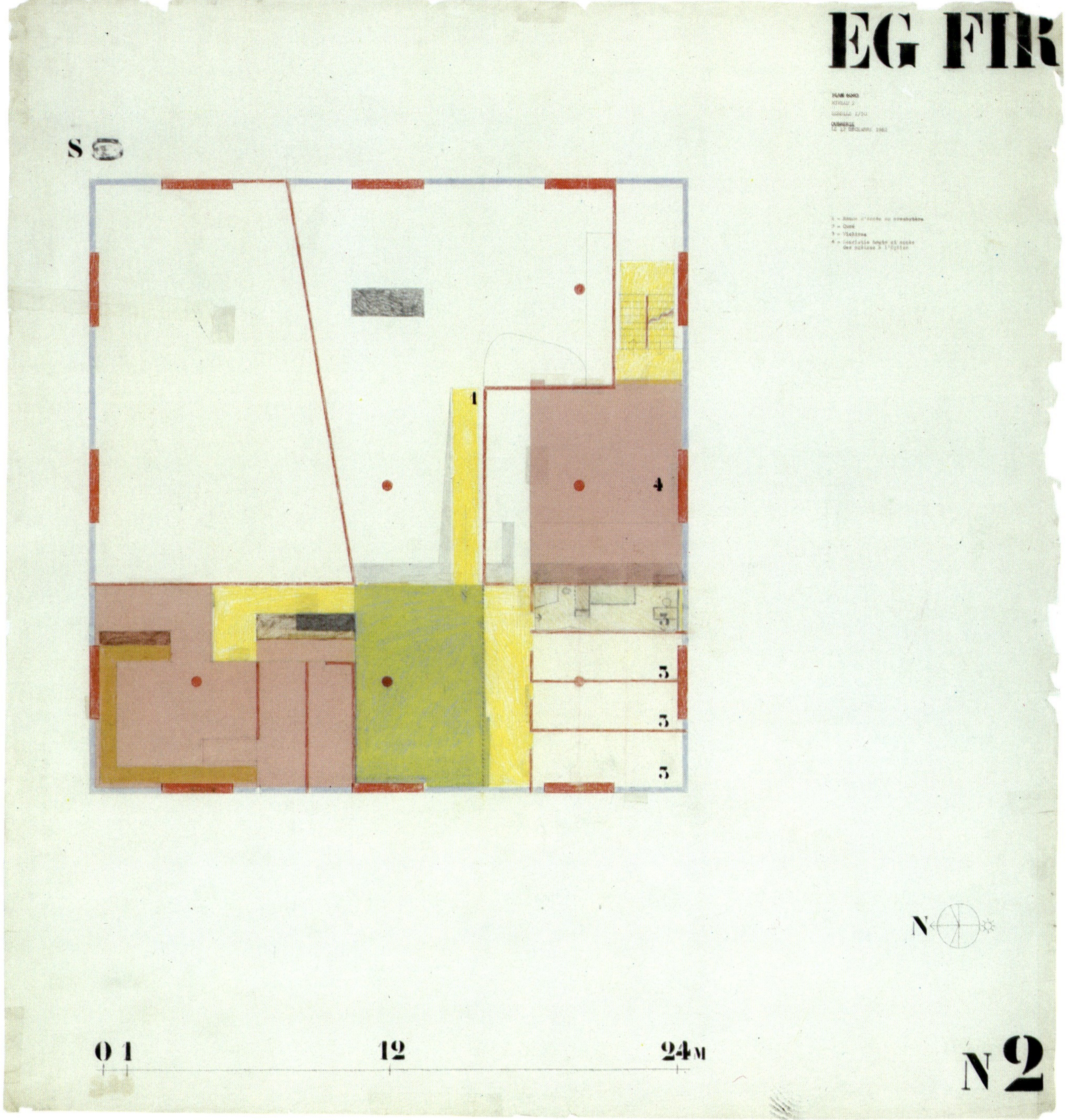

77

74

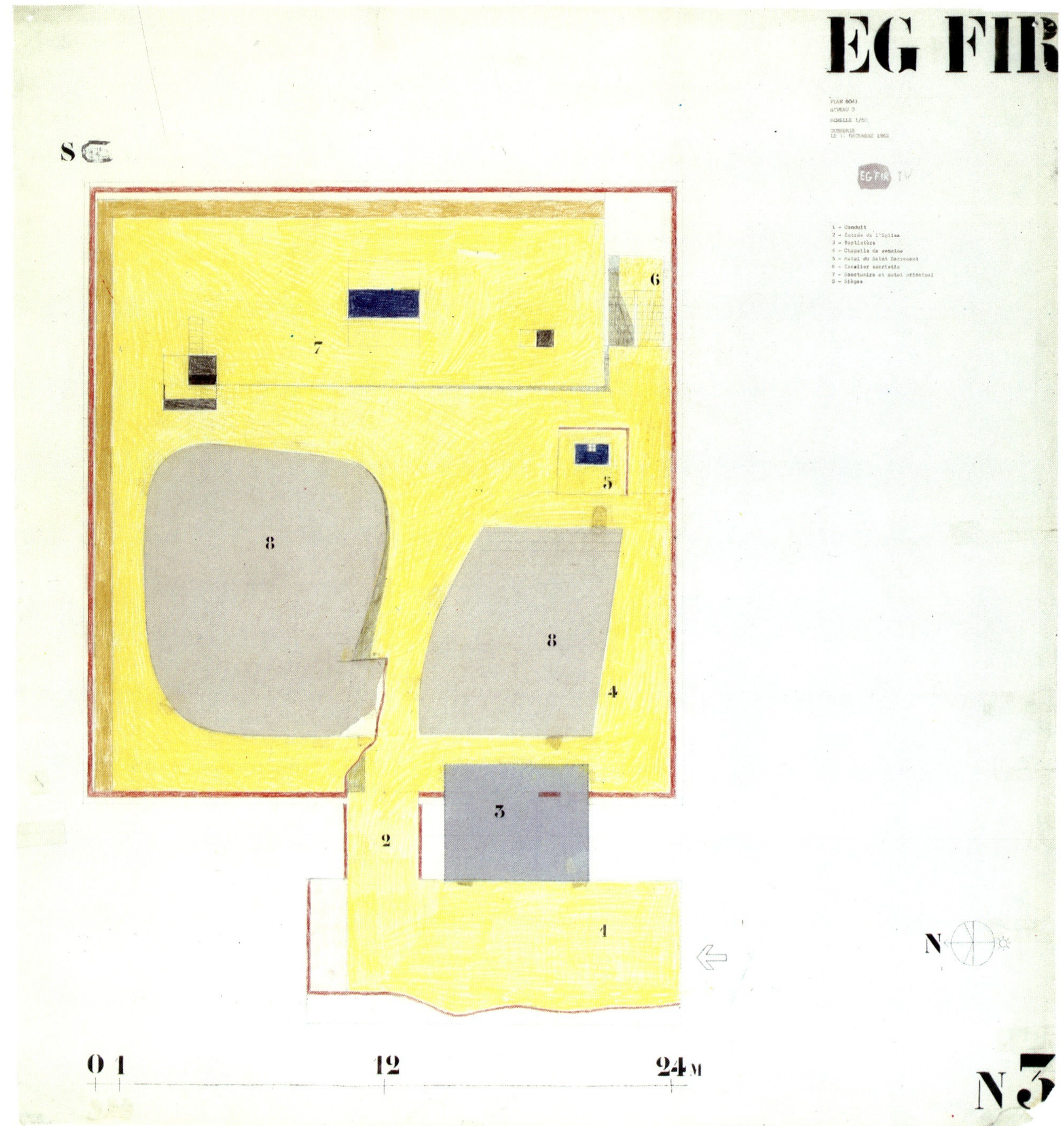
EG FIR
ECHELLE 1/50
1 - Conduit
2 - Entrée de l'Eglise
3 - Baptistère
4 - Chapelle de semaine
5 - Autel du Saint Sacrement
6 - Escalier sacristie
7 - Sanctuaire et autel principal
8 - Sièges
S
N
0 1
12
24 M
N 3

78 F.C., December 12, 1962. Jose Oubrerie in Atelier Le Corbusier. Fourth level plan. Pencil, paper. 35×36. (Pl. no. 6041.)

79 F.C., December 12, 1962. Jose Oubrerie in Atelier Le Corbusier. Fourth level plan. Pencil, paper. 35×36. (Pl. no. 6042.)

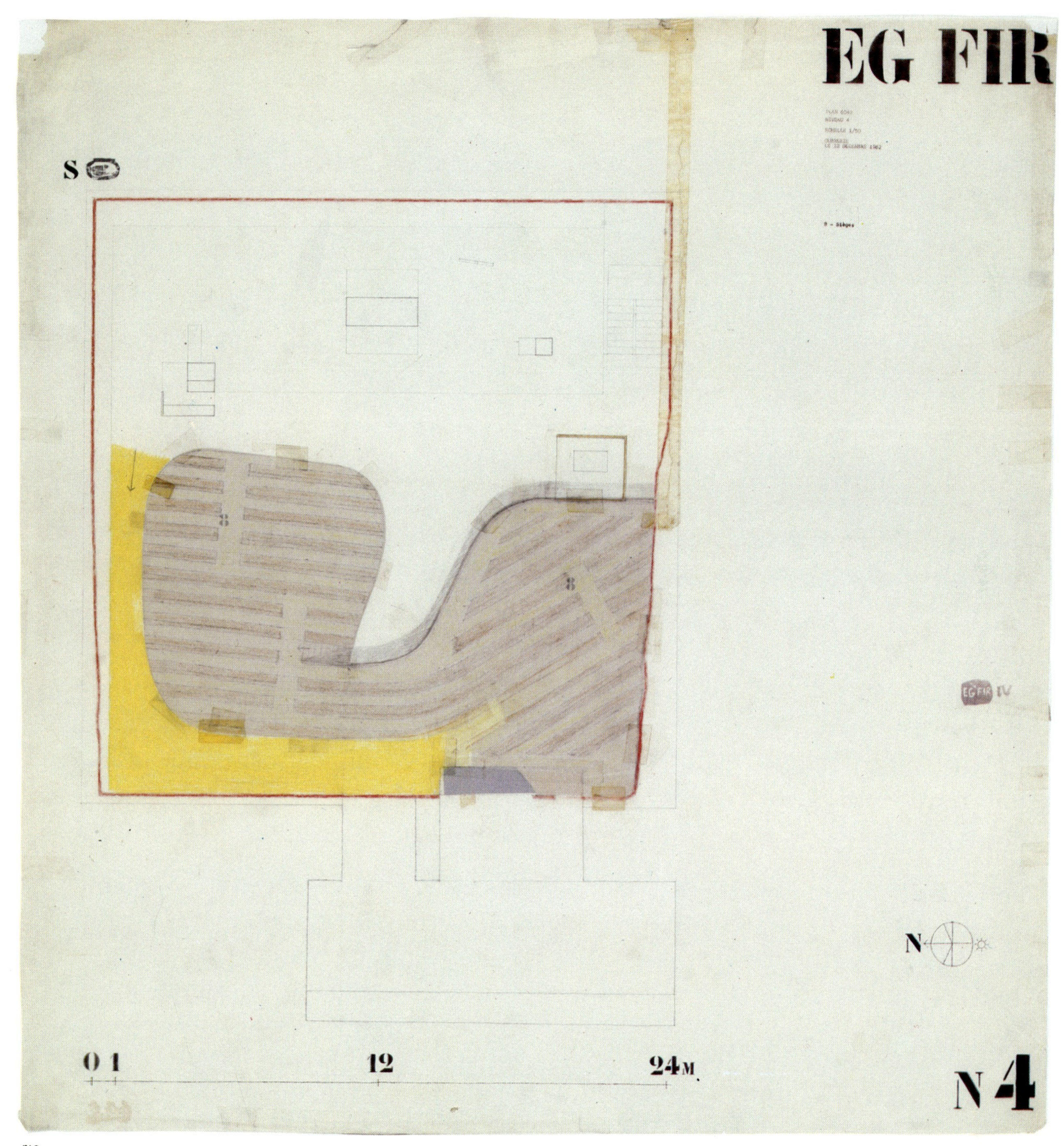

79

76

80 F.C., December 12, 1962. Jose Oubrerie in Atelier Le Corbusier. East/west section. Pencil, paper. 35×36. (Sec. no. 6043.)

81 F.C., December 12, 1962. Jose Oubrerie in Atelier Le Corbusier. North/south section. Pencil, paper. 35×36. (Sec. no. 6046.)

81

78

82 F.C., December 12, 1962. Jose Oubrerie in Atelier Le Corbusier. South/north section. Pencil, paper. 35×36. (Sec. no. 6047.)

83 F.C., September 19, 1963. Le Corbusier. Site perspective. Ink, draft paper. 16 5/16×15 1/4.

83

84 F.C., December 23, 1963. Jose Oubrerie in Atelier Le Corbusier. Fourth stage, final drawings; view from above. Ink, draft paper. 4 15/16×20 7/8.

1 footpath from Firminy-Vert
2 access to church square
3 entrance to church
4 entrance to presbytery
5 future location of swimming pool
6 rocks and stadium

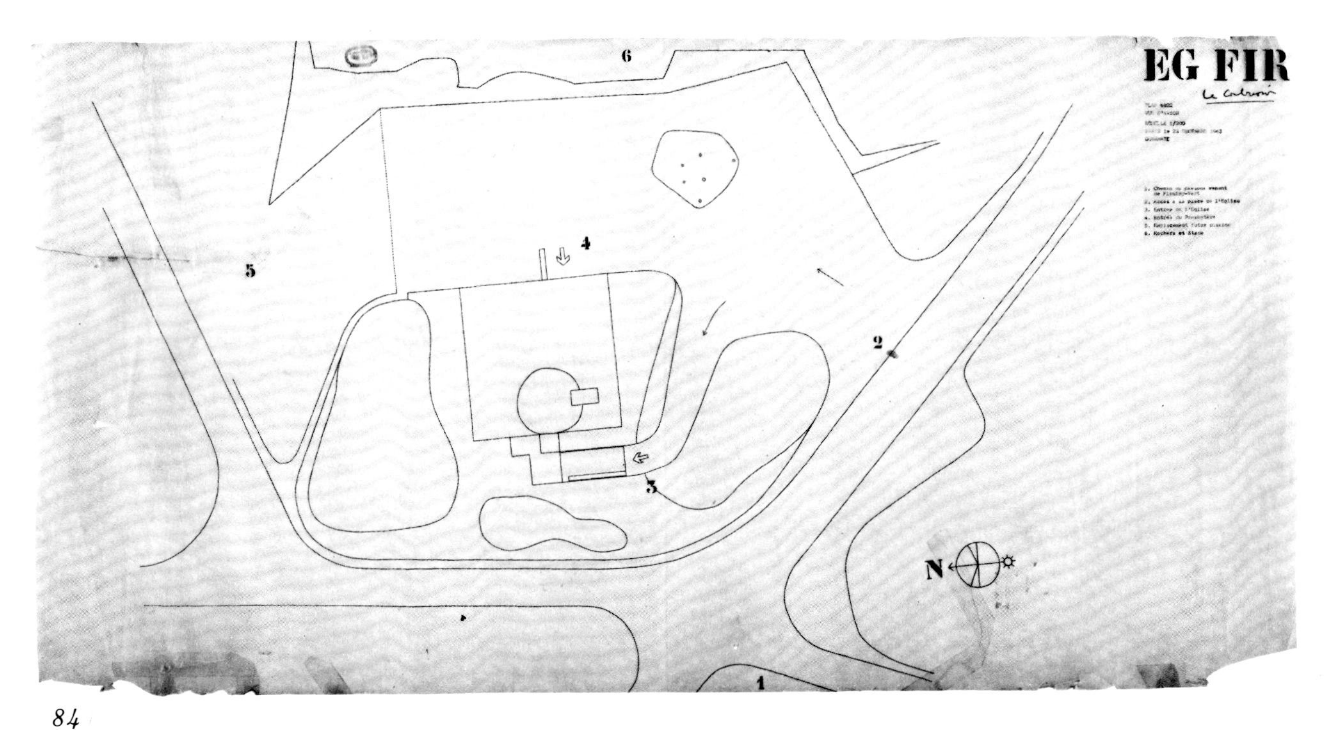

84

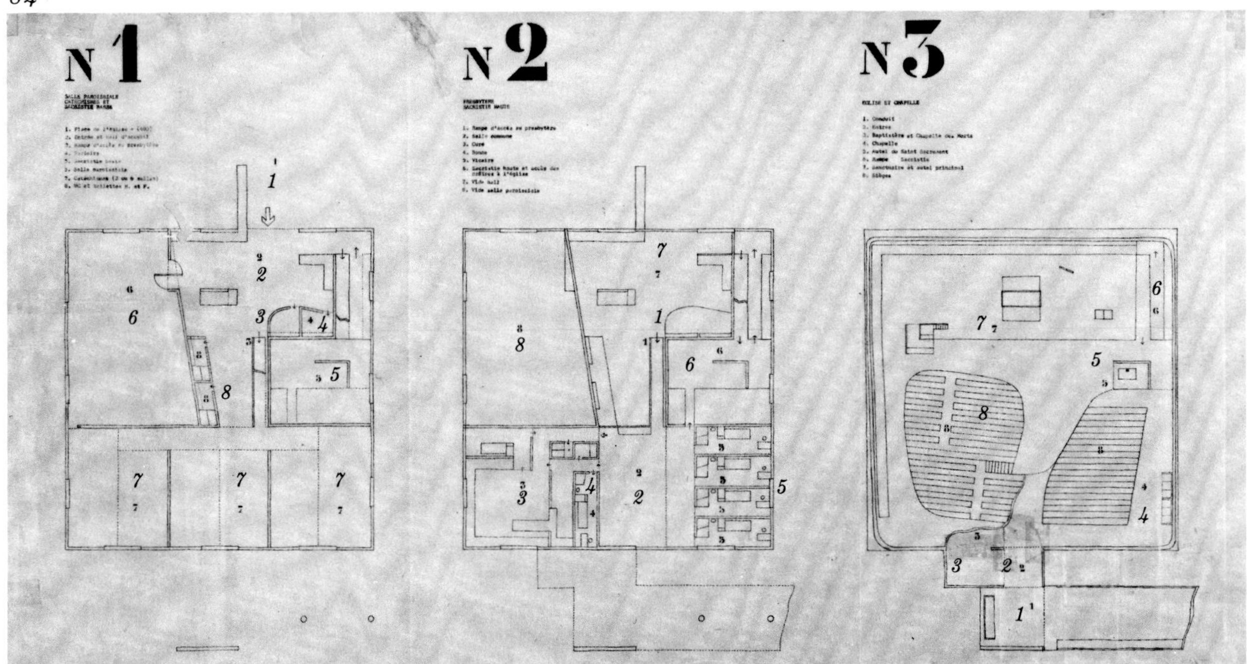

85

86 F.C., December 23, 1963. Jose Oubrerie in Atelier Le Corbusier. Section. Ink, draft paper. 35 3/4×20 7/8. (Sec. no. 6104.)

87 F.C., December 23, 1963. Jose Oubrerie in Atelier Le Corbusier. Fifth elevation. Ink, draft paper. 35 3/4×20 7/8. (Elev. no. 6105.)

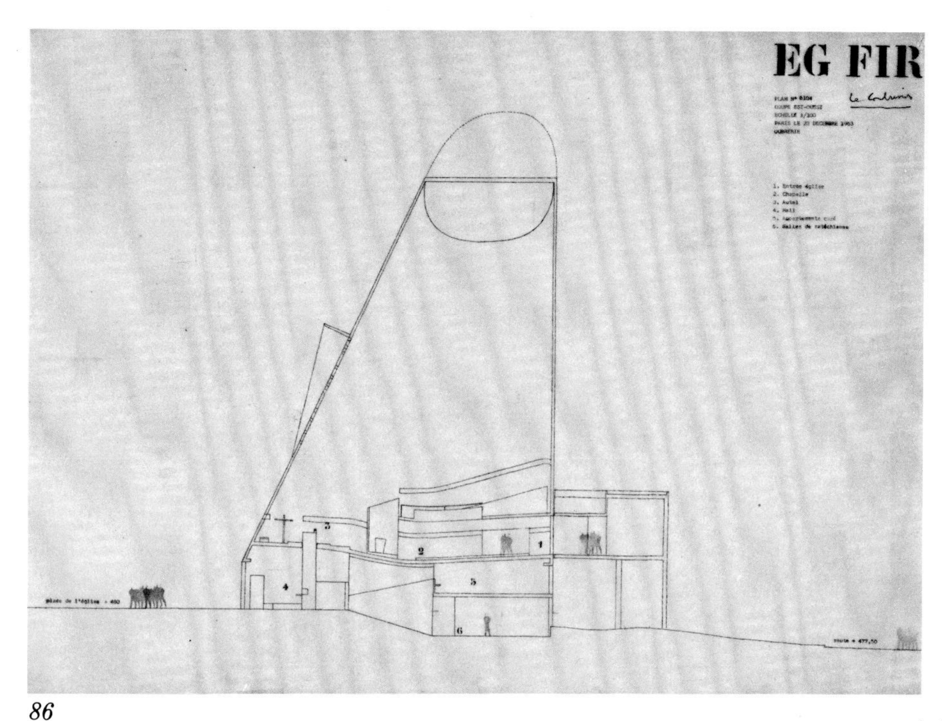

86

87

85 F.C., December 23, 1963. Jose Oubrerie in Atelier Le Corbusier. First, second and third level plans. Ink, draft paper. 57 3/8×20 7/8. (Pl. no. 6103.)

N 1
1 church square
2 entrance hall
3 access ramp to presbytery
4 confessionals
5 lower sacristy
6 parish hall
7 catechism (three or six rooms)
8 toilets

N 2
1 access ramp to presbytery
2 common room
3 priest
4 maid
5 vicar
6 upper sacristy and priest's access to church
7 open to entrance hall
8 open to parish hall

N 3
1 vestibule
2 entrance
3 baptistry and mortuary
4 chapel
5 altar of holy sacrament
6 ramp to sacristy
7 sanctuary and main altar
8 seats

82

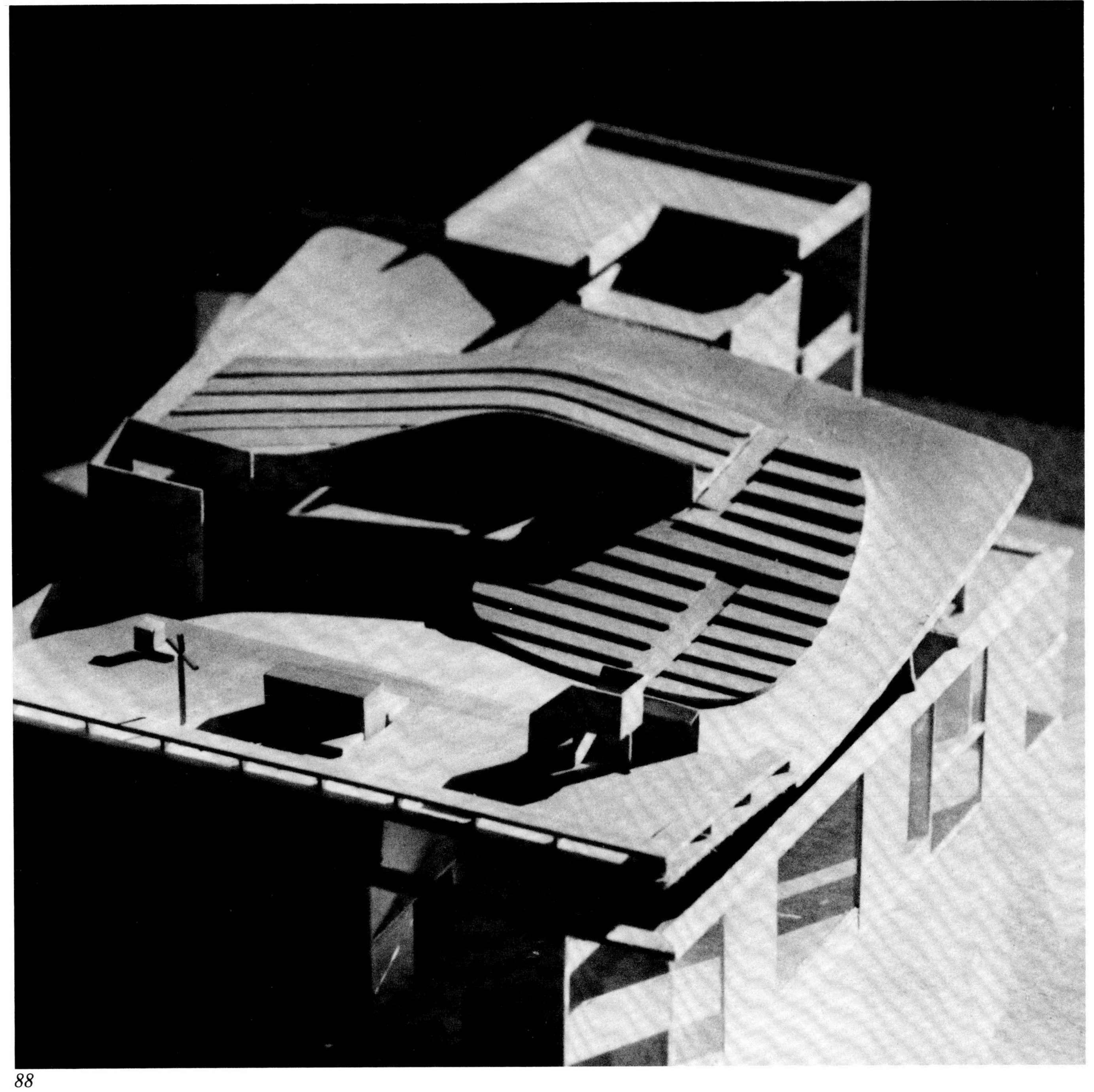

88

88 F.C., December 23, 1963. Dirlik. Final model, fourth and fifth levels. Wood.

89 F.C., December 23, 1963. Dirlik. Model, west facade: ramp and porch. Wood.

90 F.C., December 23, 1963. Dirlik. Final model. Wood.

89

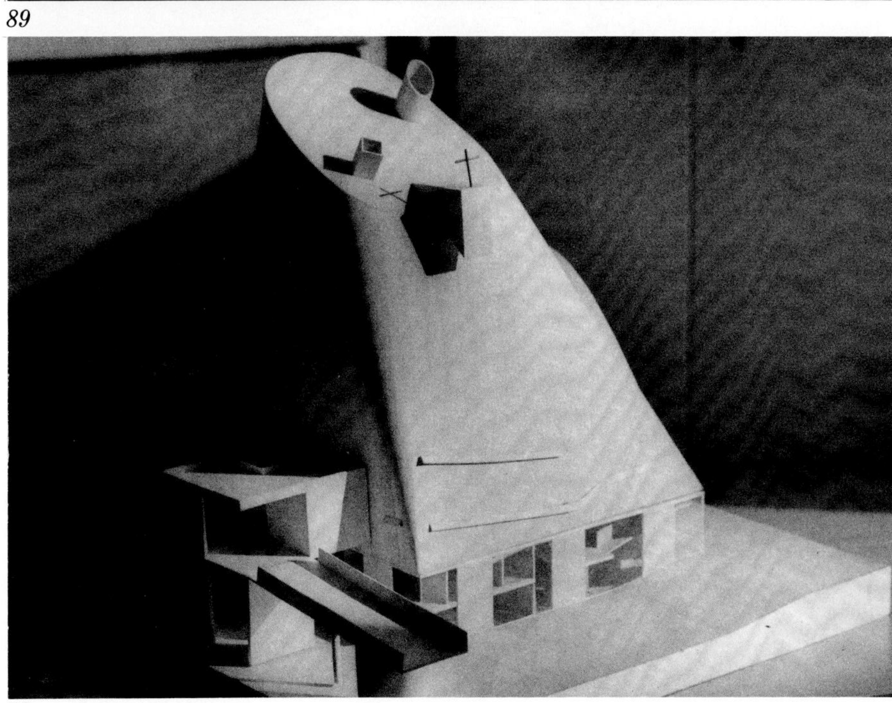

90

84 *91 F.C., September 1964.*
Le Corbusier. Member's card, Firminy Church Friends Association, second sketch. Pencil, envelope, colored paper. 13×18.

92 F.C., November 3, 1964. Le Corbusier. First print of a lithograph made to raise funds for the Church. (Original collage, July 26, 1964. Le Corbusier.) 16 5/16×15 1/4. (Detail.)

93 F.C., undated. Le Corbusier. Members card, first sketch. Pencil, paper, colored paper. 4 1/8×6 1/2.

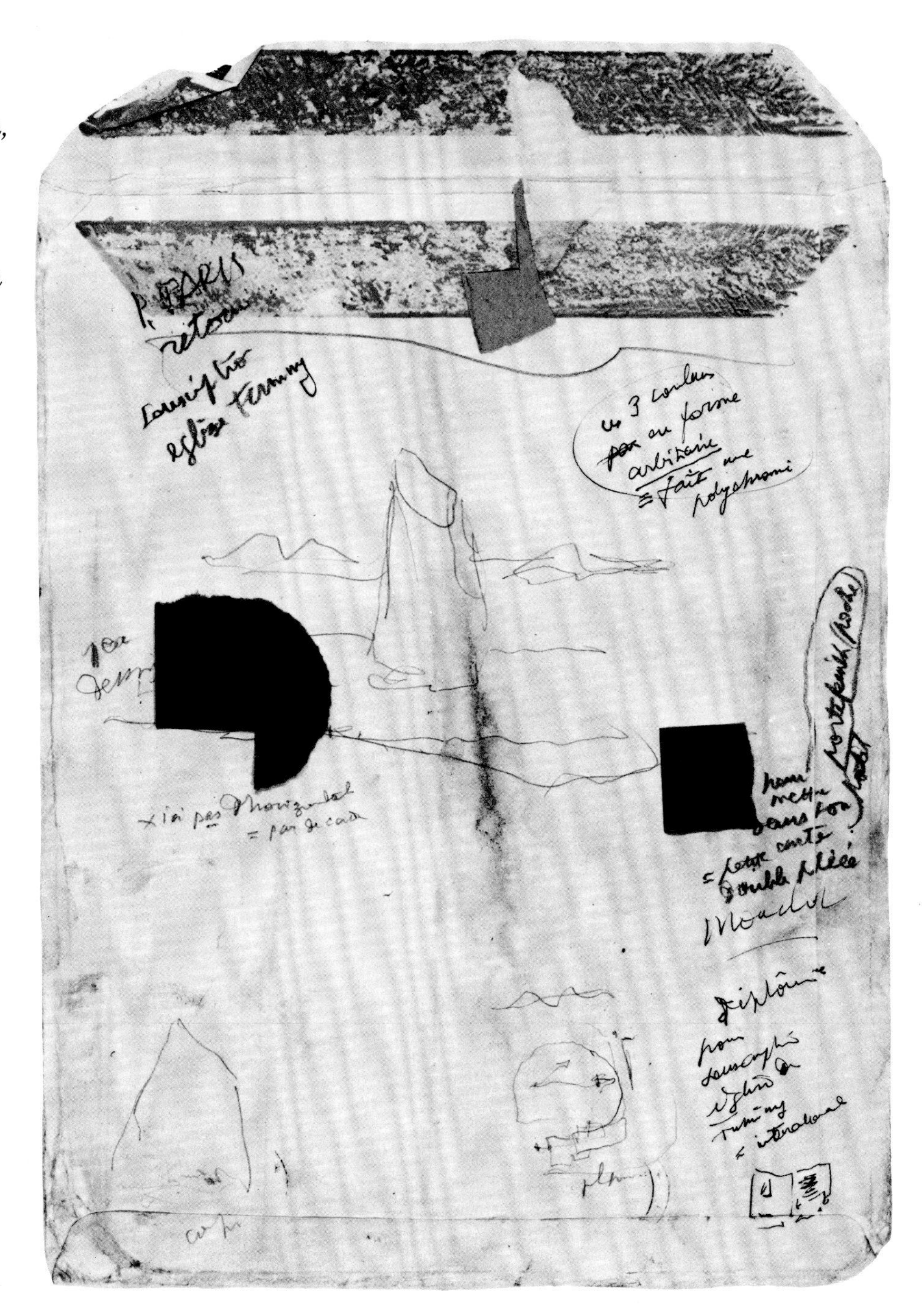

92

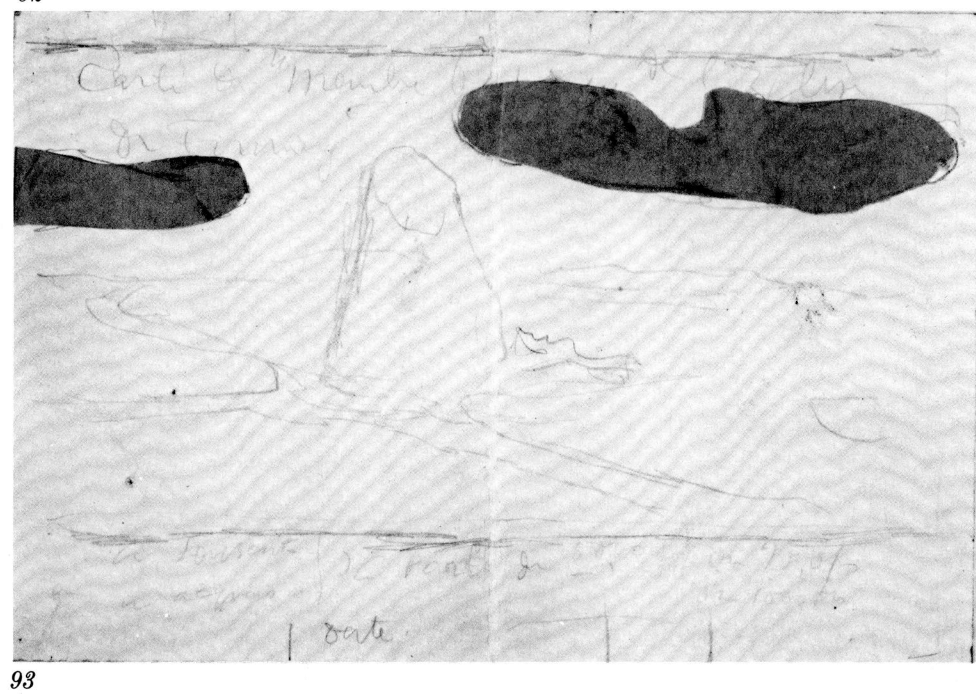

93

Late Drawings
Atelier Le Corbusier 1962-1964
Atelier Oubrerie 1970-1979

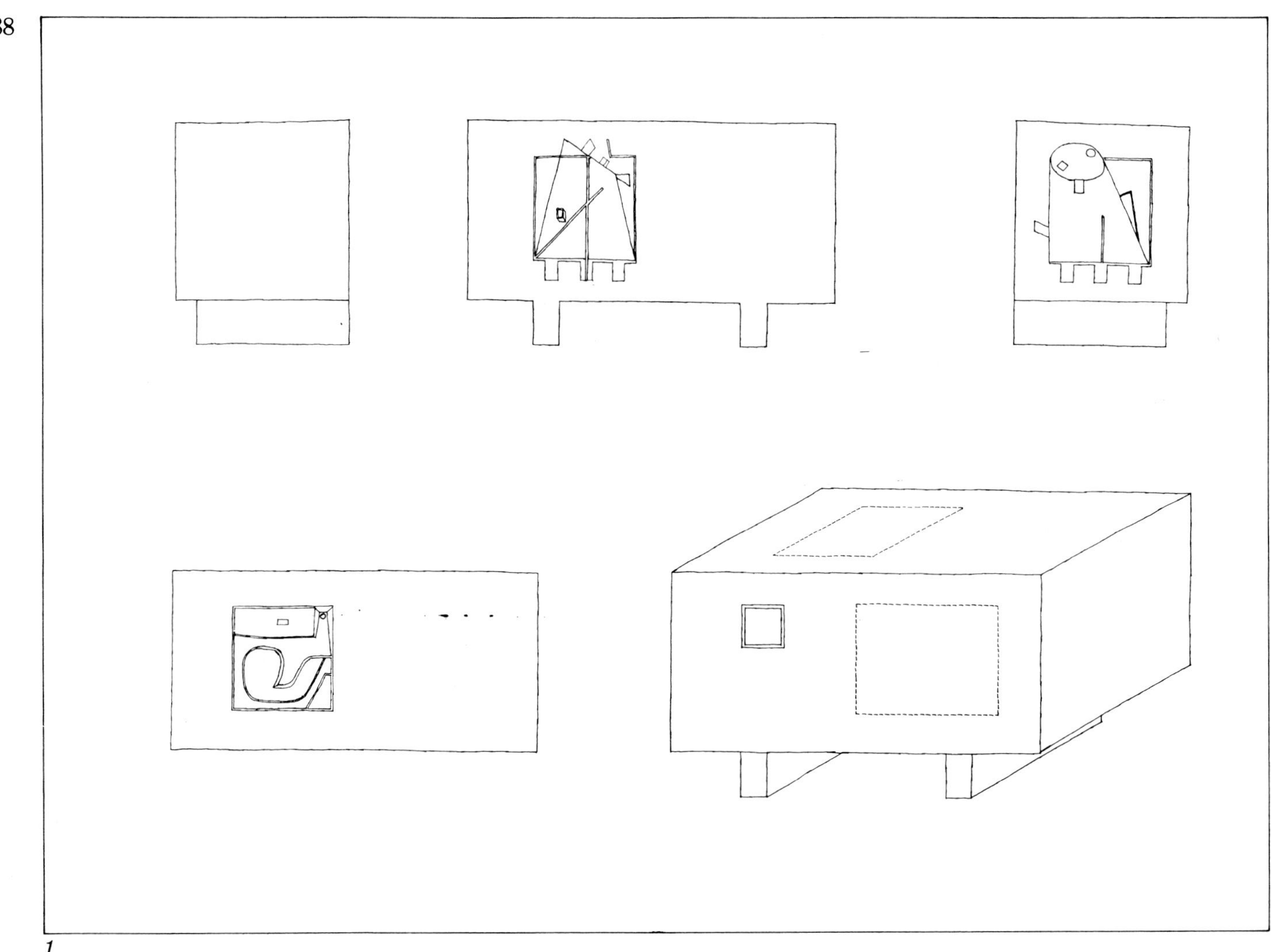

1

1 F.C., March 5, 1970. Atelier Jose Oubrerie. Cornerstone. Ink, draft paper. 28×20 1/2.

2 F.C., March 5, 1970. Atelier Jose Oubrerie. Monument for foundation ceremony. 28×20 1/2.

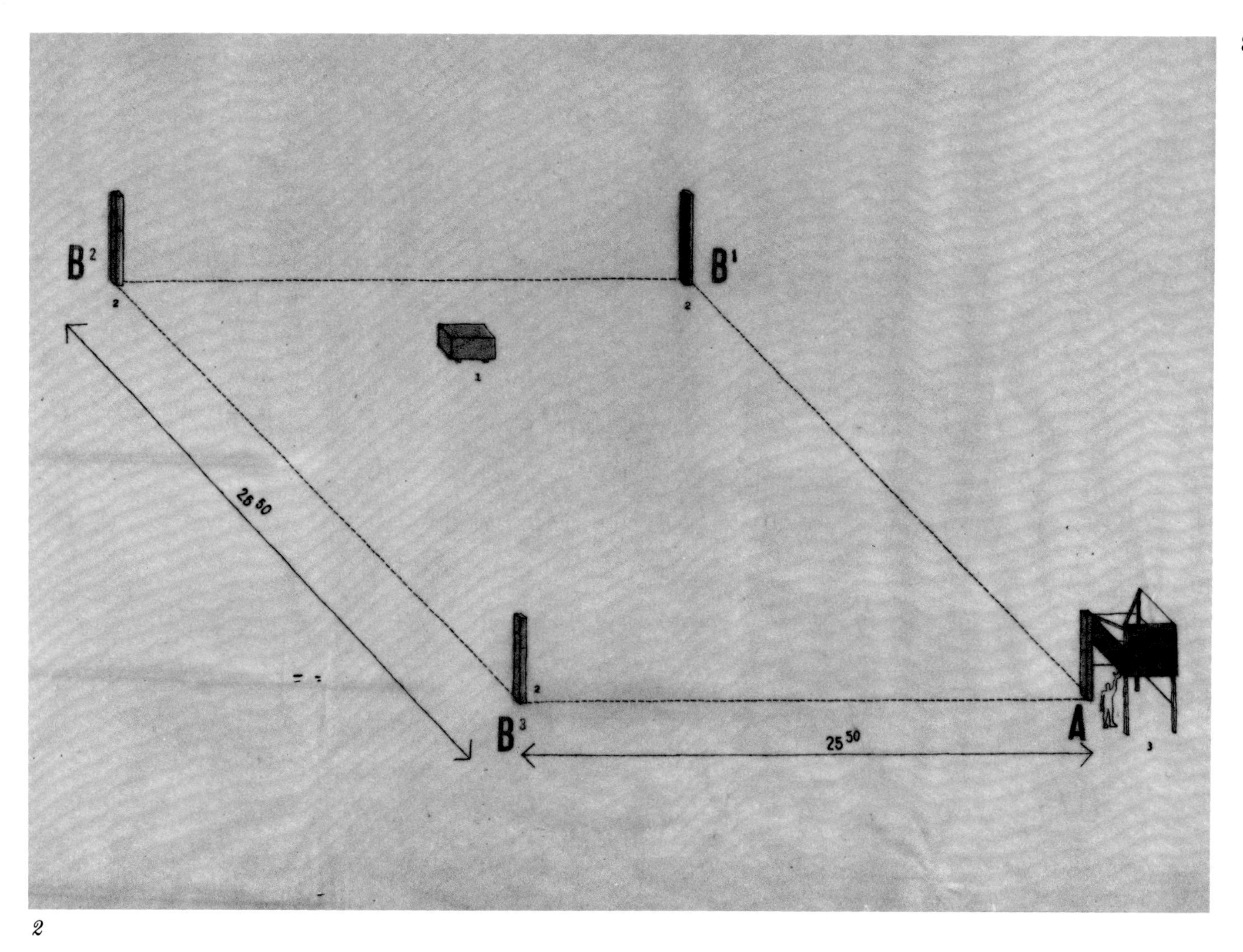

2

3

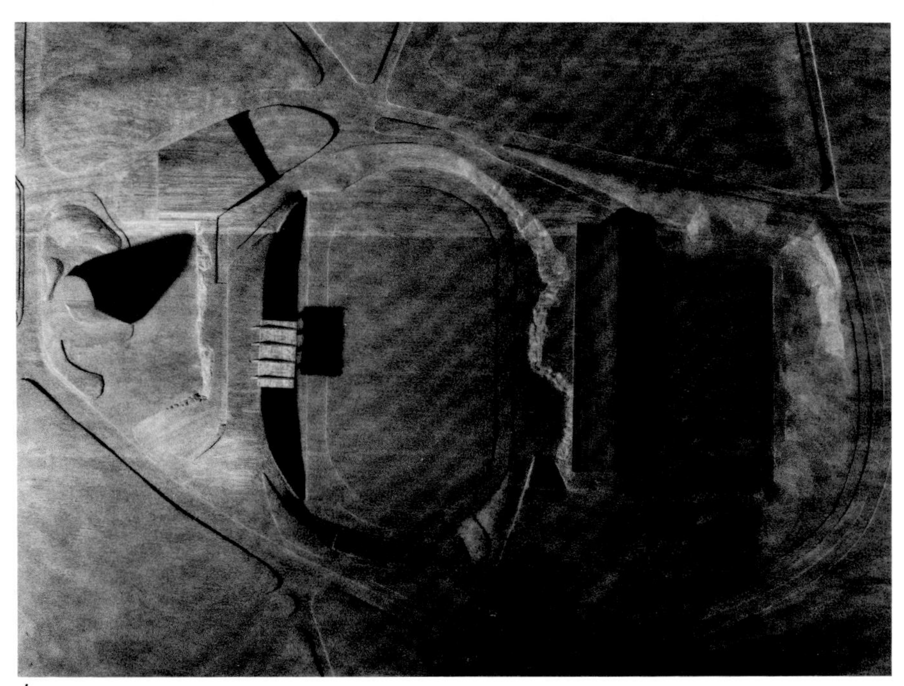

4

3 F.C., September 1980. Atelier Jose Oubrerie, School of Architecture, University of Kentucky, Lexington (Jean Cecil, Tai Choi). Site model, view looking east. Carved mahogany.

4 F.C., September 1980. Atelier Jose Oubrerie, School of Architecture, University of Kentucky, Lexington. Site model, general view from above.

5 F.C., September 1980. Atelier Jose Oubrerie, School of Architecture, University of Kentucky, Lexington. Site model, view looking west.

6 F.C., October 27, 1970. Atelier Jose Oubrerie, Fonti, Stagno, Wagner. West section on site. Ink, collage. (Sec. no. 569.)

5

6

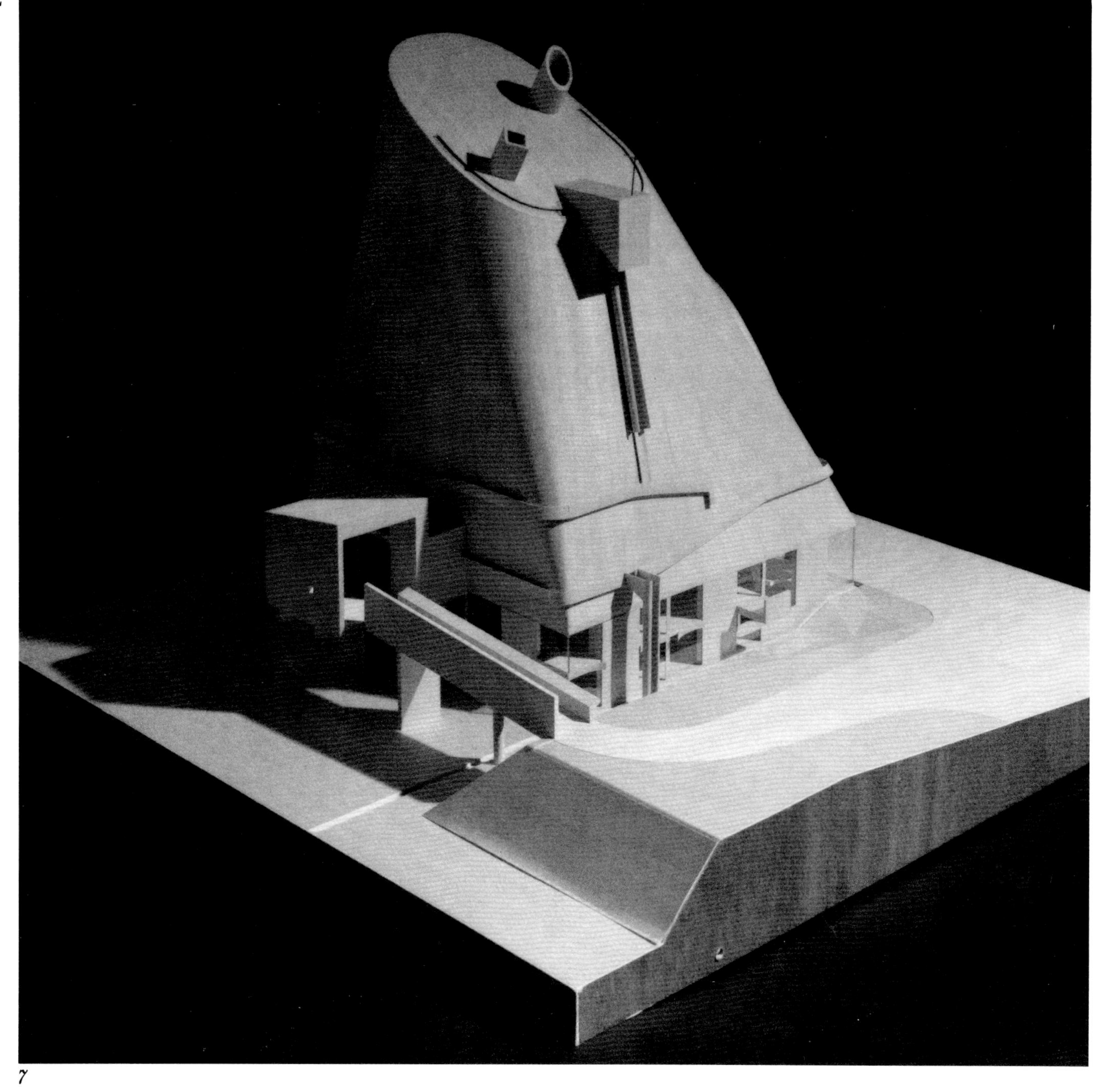

7

7 F.C., October 27, 1970. Atelier Jose Oubrerie, Fonti, Stagno, Wagner. Study model, West facade. Wood painted white.

8 F.C., February 28, 1974. Atelier Jose Oubrerie. Final site implementation. Pencil, draft paper. 28×35. (Pl. no. 7000.)

1 church square
2 contemplation pit
3 church ramp
4 hill

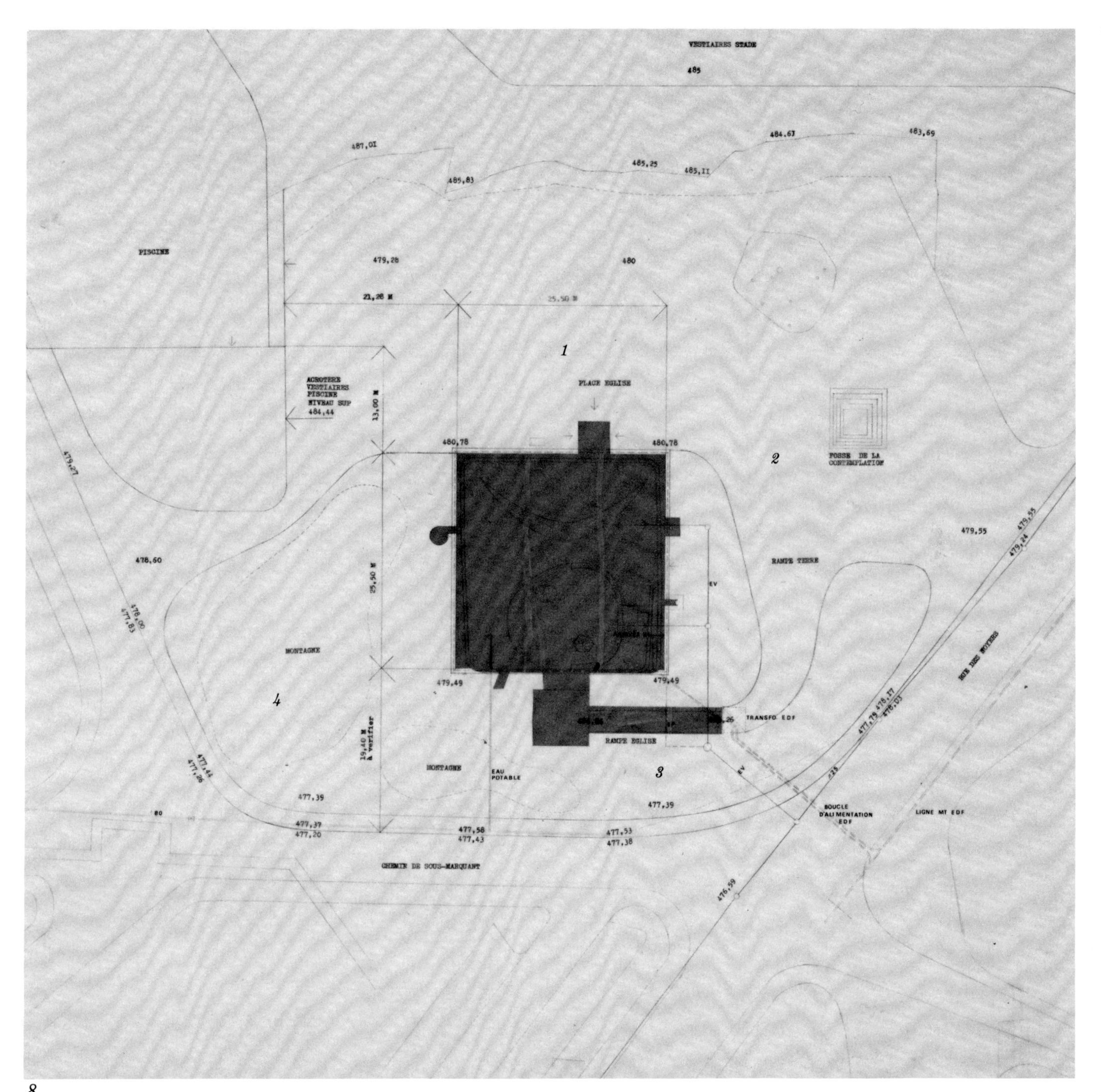

8

1 presbytery ramp
2 bridge
3 priests' entrance
4 stair to fourth level
5 kitchen
6 dining
7 priests' quarters
8 priests' room
9 toilet
10 employee's room
11 office waiting room
12 secretary
13 office
14 sacristy
15 ramp to second and fourth levels
16 balcony

94

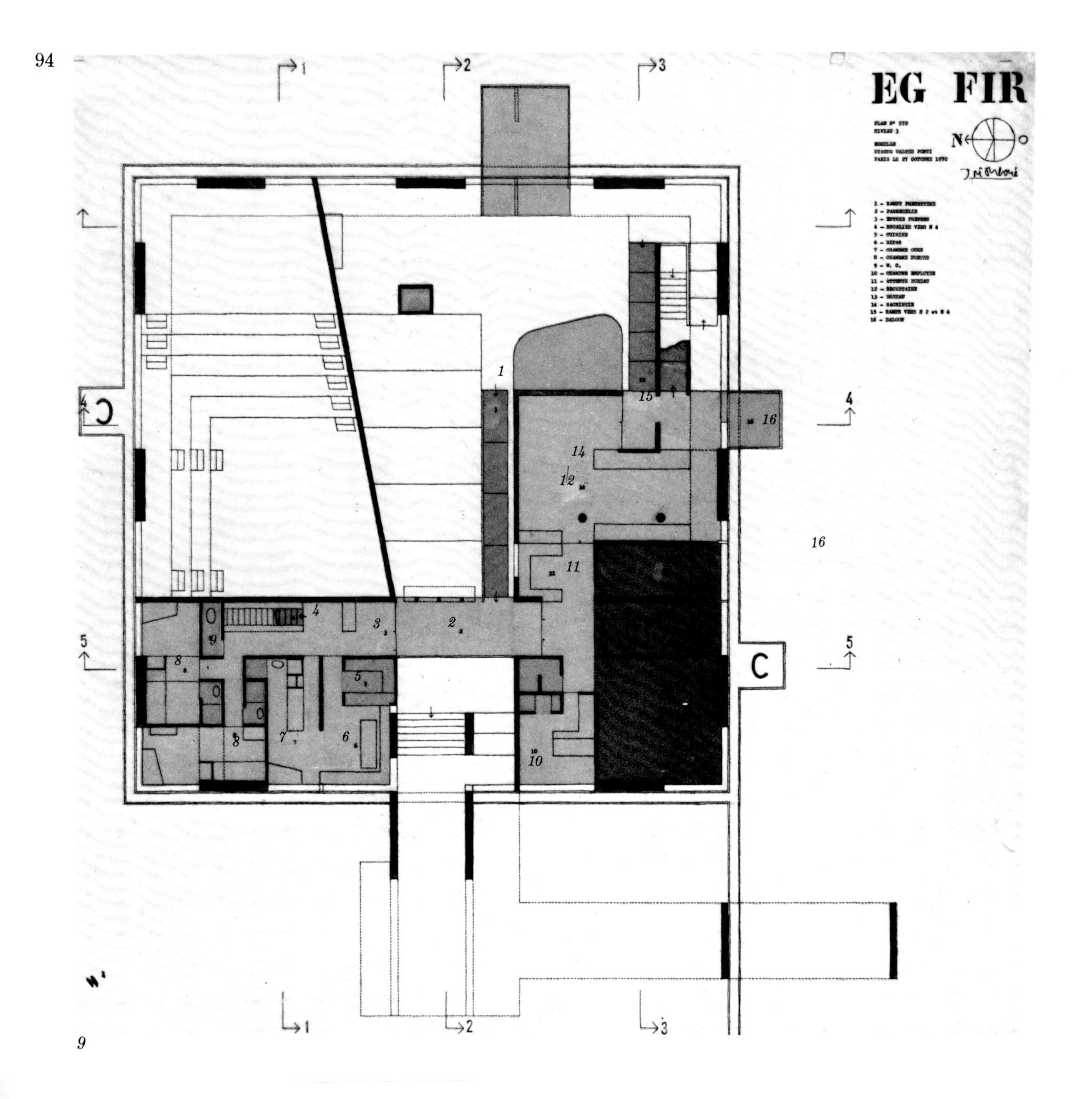

9

9 F.C., October 27, 1970. Atelier Jose Oubrerie, Fonti, Stagno, Wagner. First level plan. Ink, collage. 34×33 7/8. (Pl. no. 570.)

10 F.C., October 27, 1970. Atelier Jose Oubrerie, Fonti, Stagno, Wagner. Second level plan. Ink, collage. 34×33 7/8. (Pl. no. 571.)

1 church square
2 entry porch
3 interior ramp to first level
4 ramped access to presbytery, no. 3
5 ramp to first and third level
6 parish hall-upper level
7 coatroom
8 chemin de Ronde
9 tiers

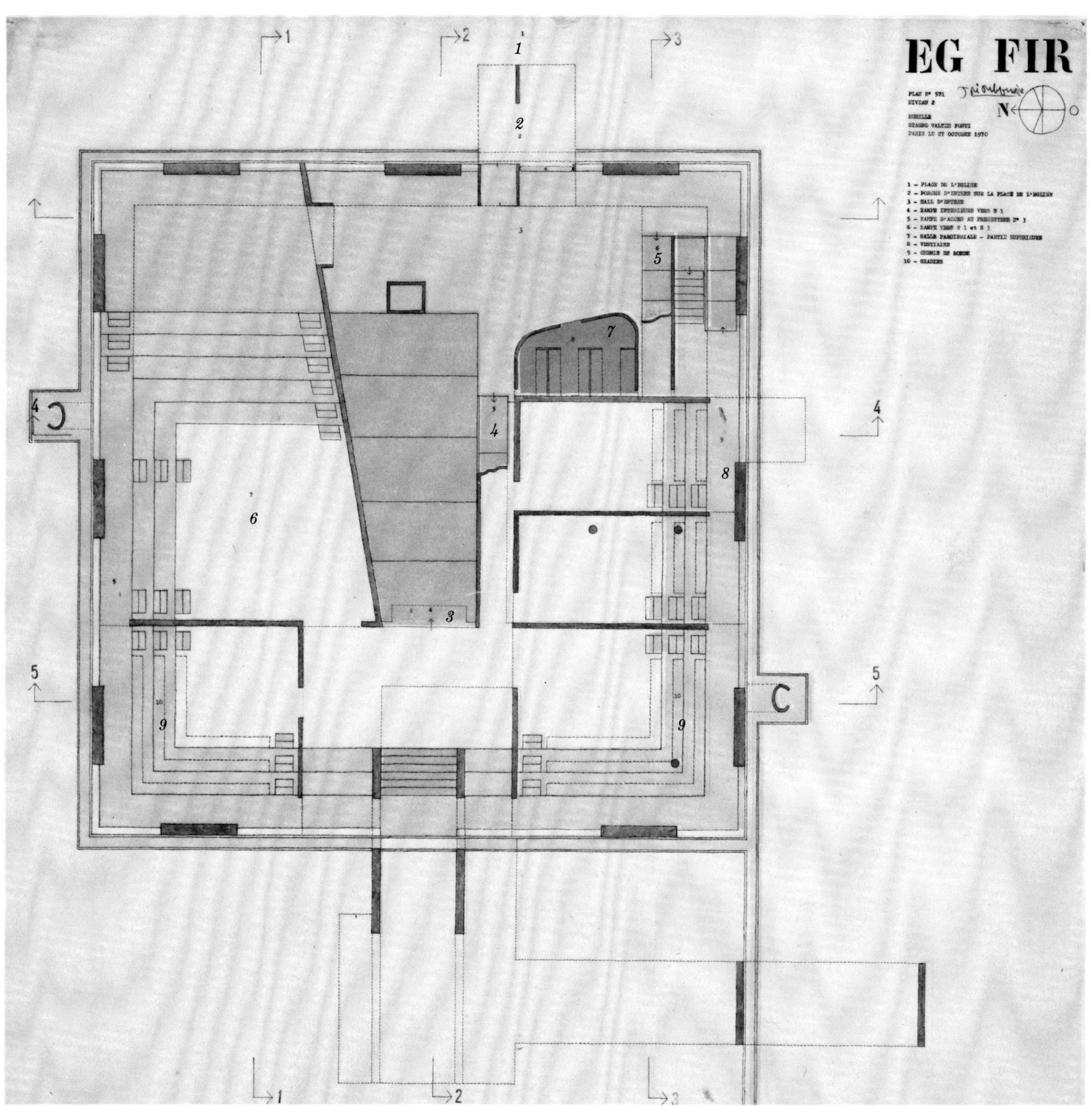

10

1 lower interior space
2 catechism meeting room, no. 1
3 catechism meeting room, no. 2
4 catechism meeting room, no. 3
5 catechism meeting room, no. 4
6 lower level, great hall
7 W.C.
8 recess
9 transformer
10 heating
11 exchanger
12 technical space under tiers
13 stair to chemin de Ronde *and second level*

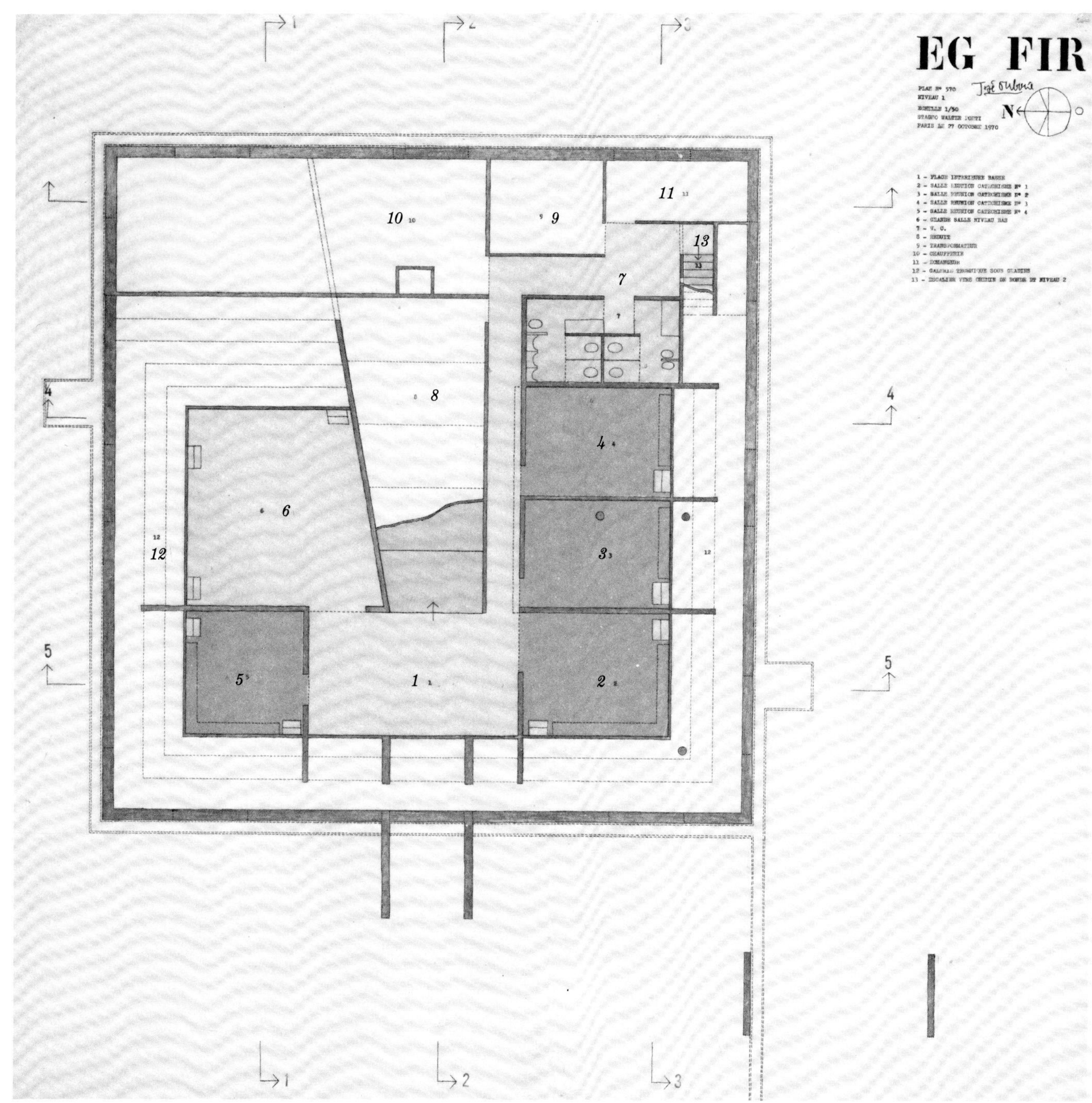

11

11 F.C., October 27, 1970. Atelier Jose Oubrerie, Fonti, Stagno, Wagner. Third level plan. Ink, collage. 34 × 33 7/8. (Pl. no. 572.)

12 F.C., October 27, 1970. Atelier Jose Oubrerie, Fonti, Stagno, Wagner. Fourth level plan. Ink, collage. 34 × 33 7/8. (Pl. no. 573.)

1 ramp
2 porch
3 main door
4 small door-entry lock
5 daily chapel
6 altar
7 seats
8 church
9 sacristy ramp
10 main altar
11 rostrum
12 president's seat
13 cross
14 space for baptism
15 priests' bench
16 offices
17 atrium
18 storage
19 staircase to third level

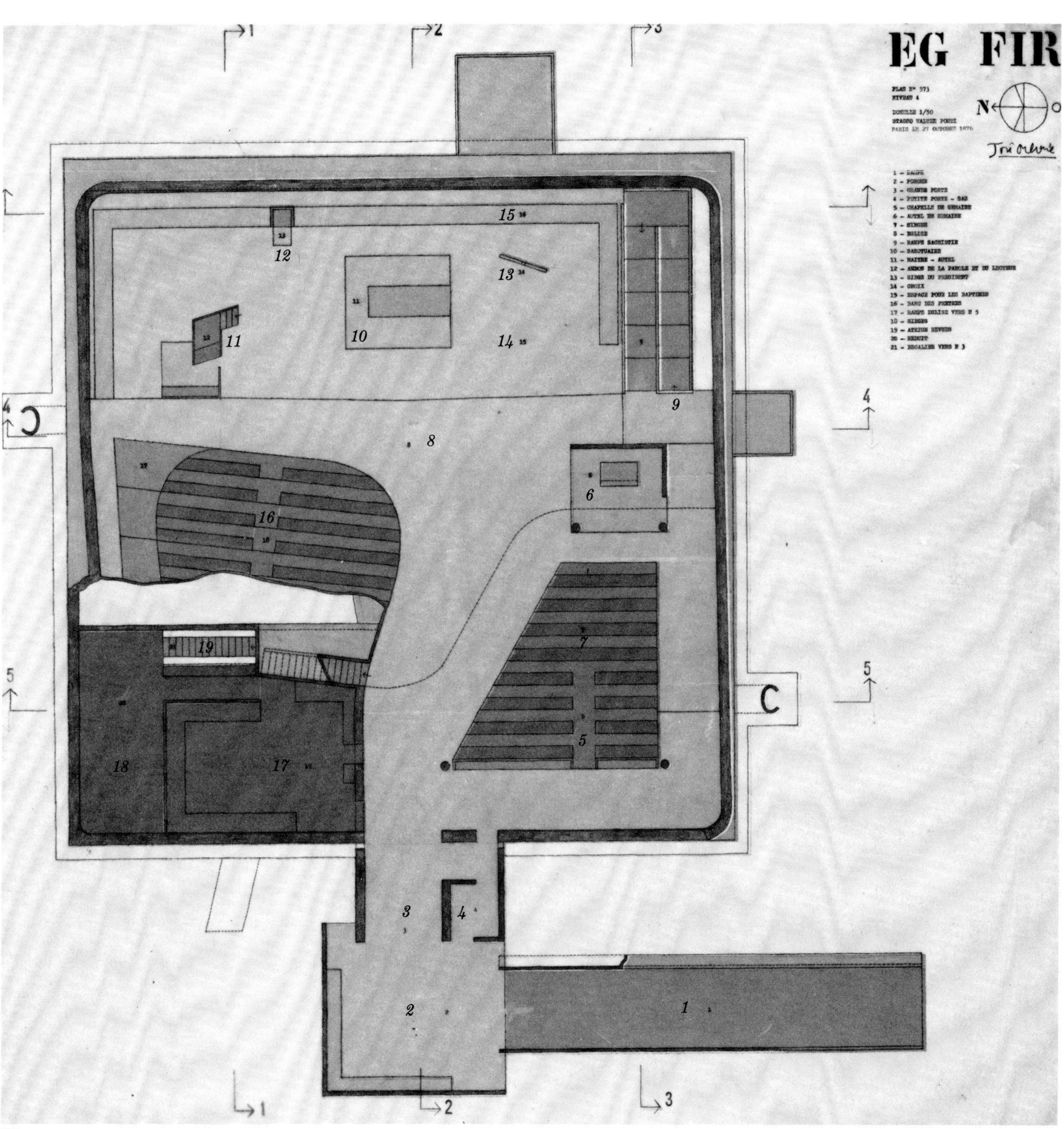

12

1 sanctuary
2 main altar
3 president's seat
4 pulpit
5 cross
6 altar daily chapel
7 ramp
8 seats
9 standing room

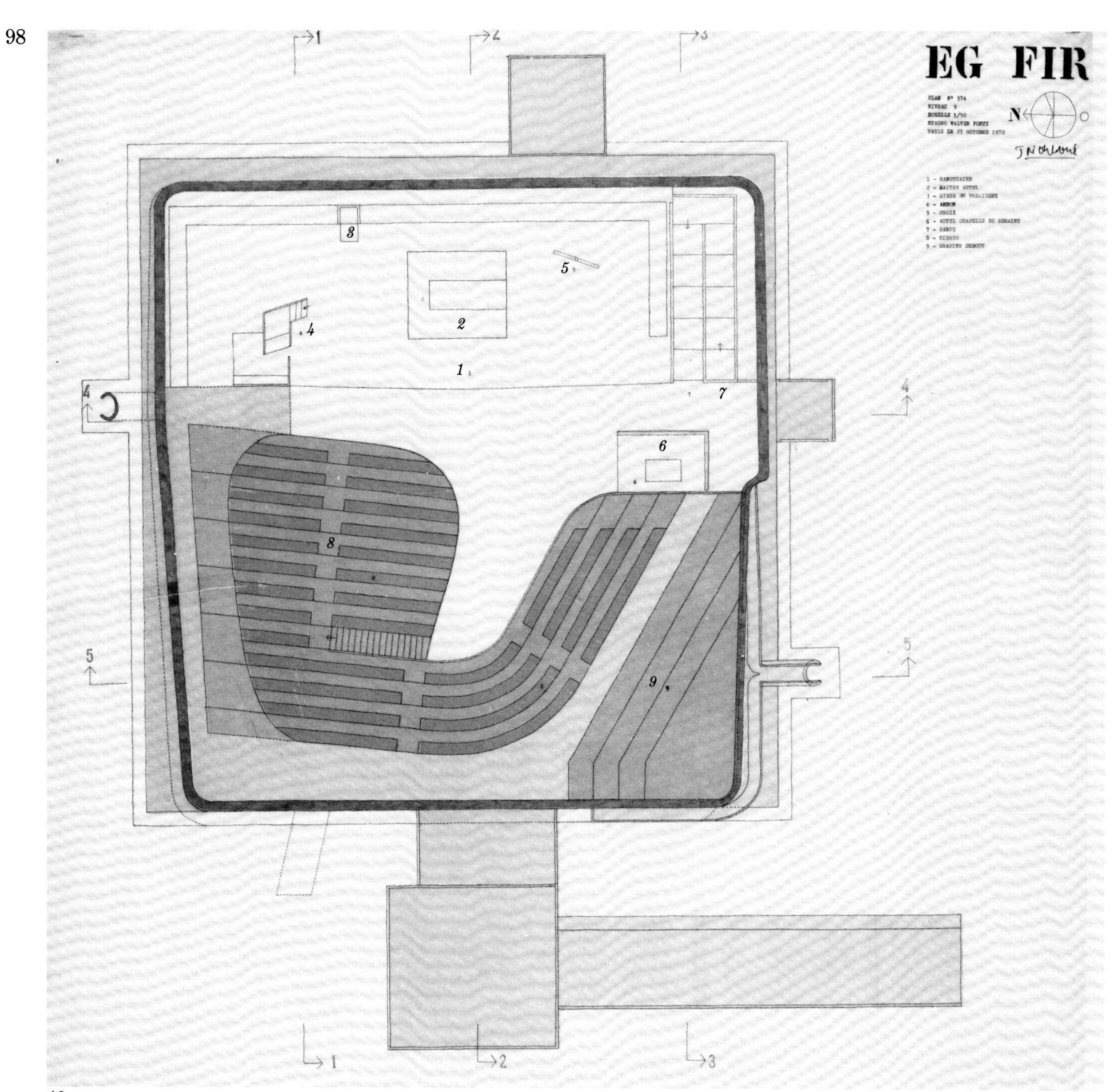

13

13 F.C., October 27, 1970. Atelier Jose Oubrerie, Fonti, Stagno, Wagner. Fifth level plan. 34 × 33 7/8. (Pl. no. 574.)

14. F.C., October 27, 1970. Atelier Jose Oubrerie, Fonti, Stagno, Wagner. First section, east/west. Ink, collage. 34 × 33 7/8. (Sec. no. 575.)

1 church square
2 great hall
3 meeting room, no. 1
4 corridor
5 priests' quarters
6 atrium
7 pulpit
8 seats
9 porch
10 canon à lumière

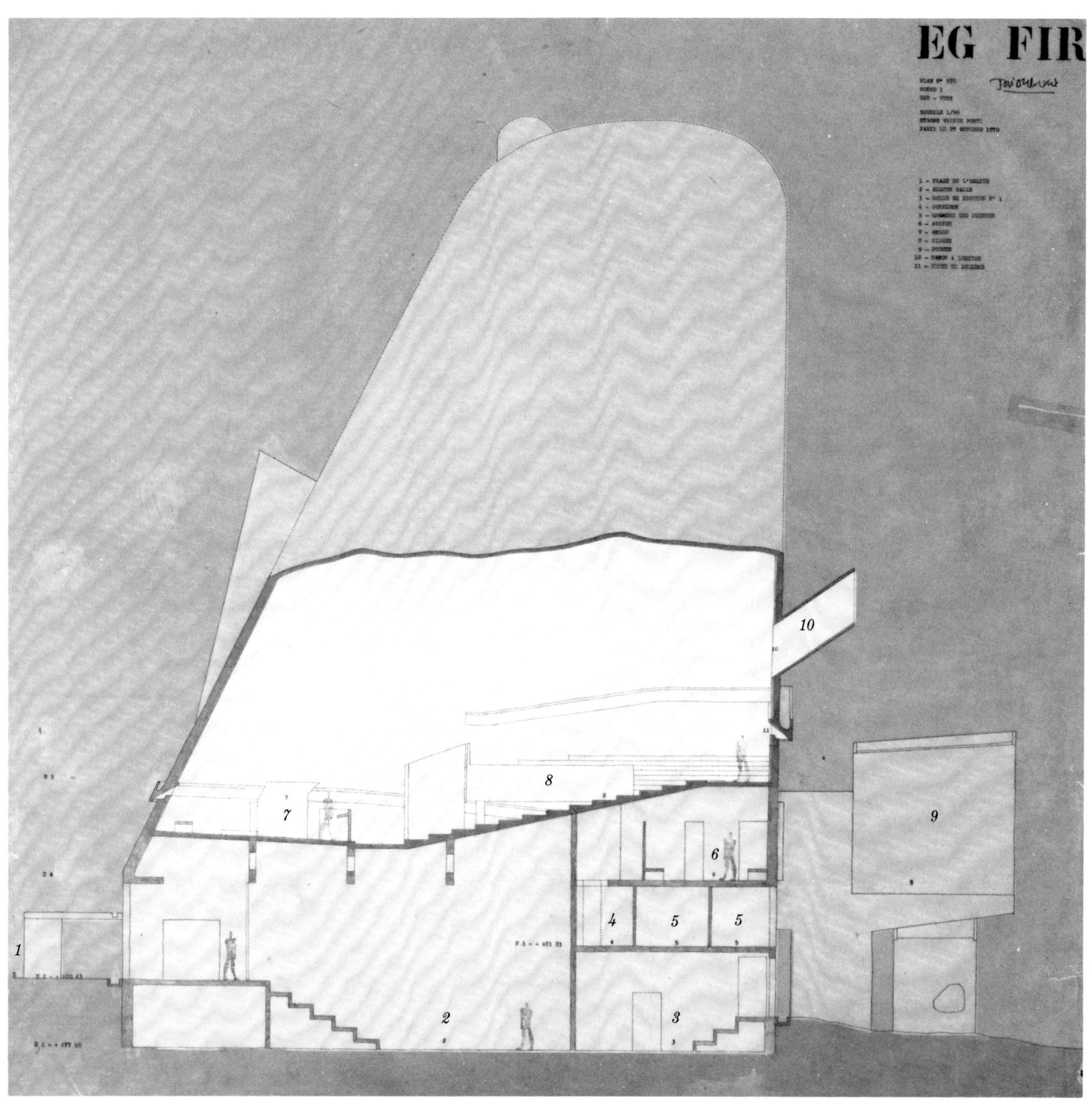

14

1 church square
2 heating
3 ramp
4 lower interior space
5 presbytery ramp
6 bridge
7 ramp to church sacristy
8 priests' bench
9 altar
10 church entrance to porch
11 seats
12 standing room
13 light slot
14 canon à lumière

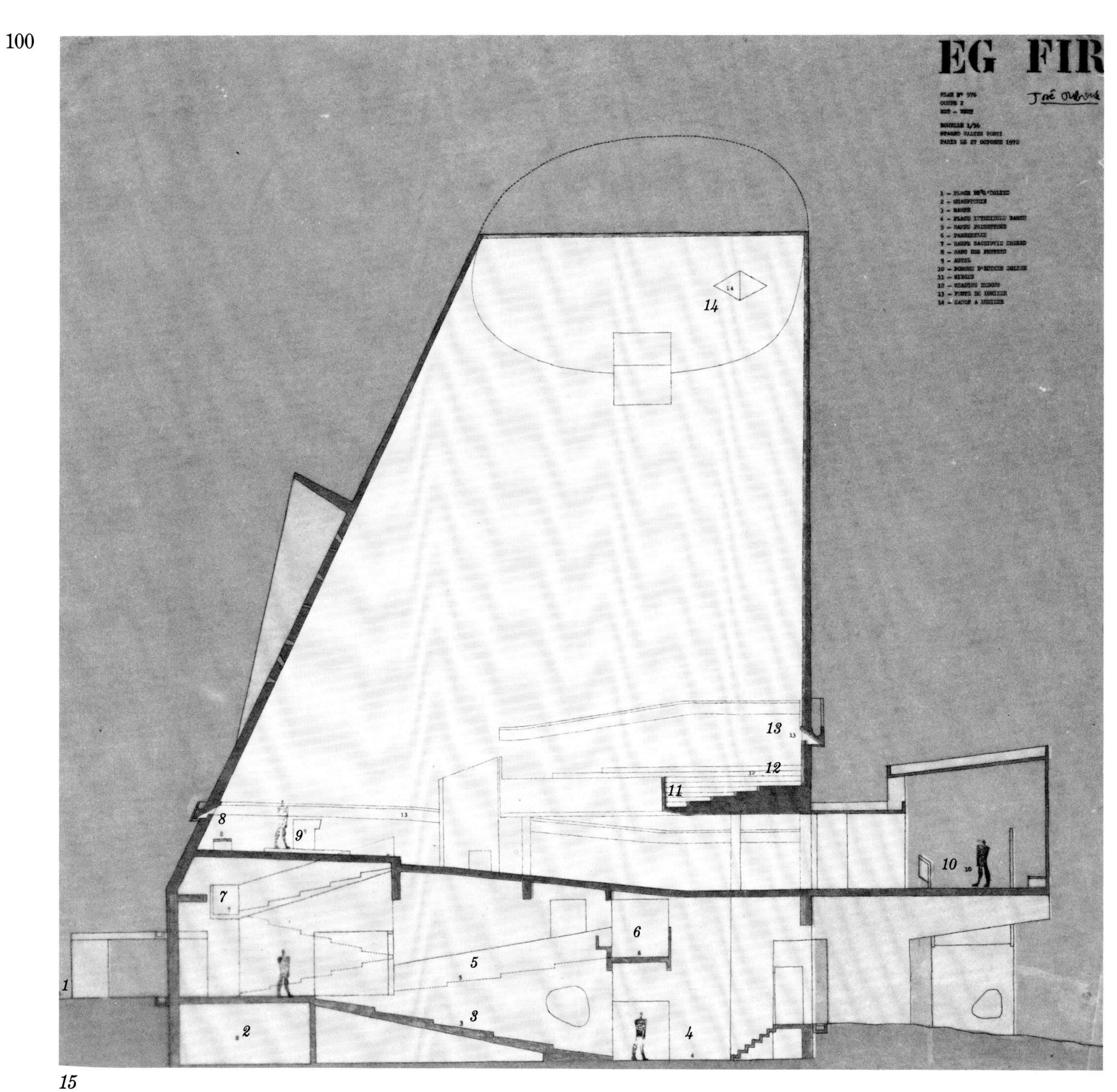

15

15 F.C., October 27, 1970. Atelier Jose Oubrerie, Fonti, Stagno, Wagner. Second section, east/west. Ink, collage. 34×33 7/8. (Sec. no. 576.)

16 F.C., October 27, 1970. Atelier Jose Oubrerie, Fonti, Stagno, Wagner. Third section, east/west. Ink, collage. 34×33 7/8. (Section no. 577.)

1 church square
2 transformer
3 corridor
4 women's room
5 catechism meeting room, no. 4
6 catechism meeting room, no. 3
7 catechism meeting room, no. 2
8 ramp to sacristy
9 sacristy
10 office
11 exterior ramp
12 altar
13 chapel
14 standing room
15 window slot
16 canon à lumière

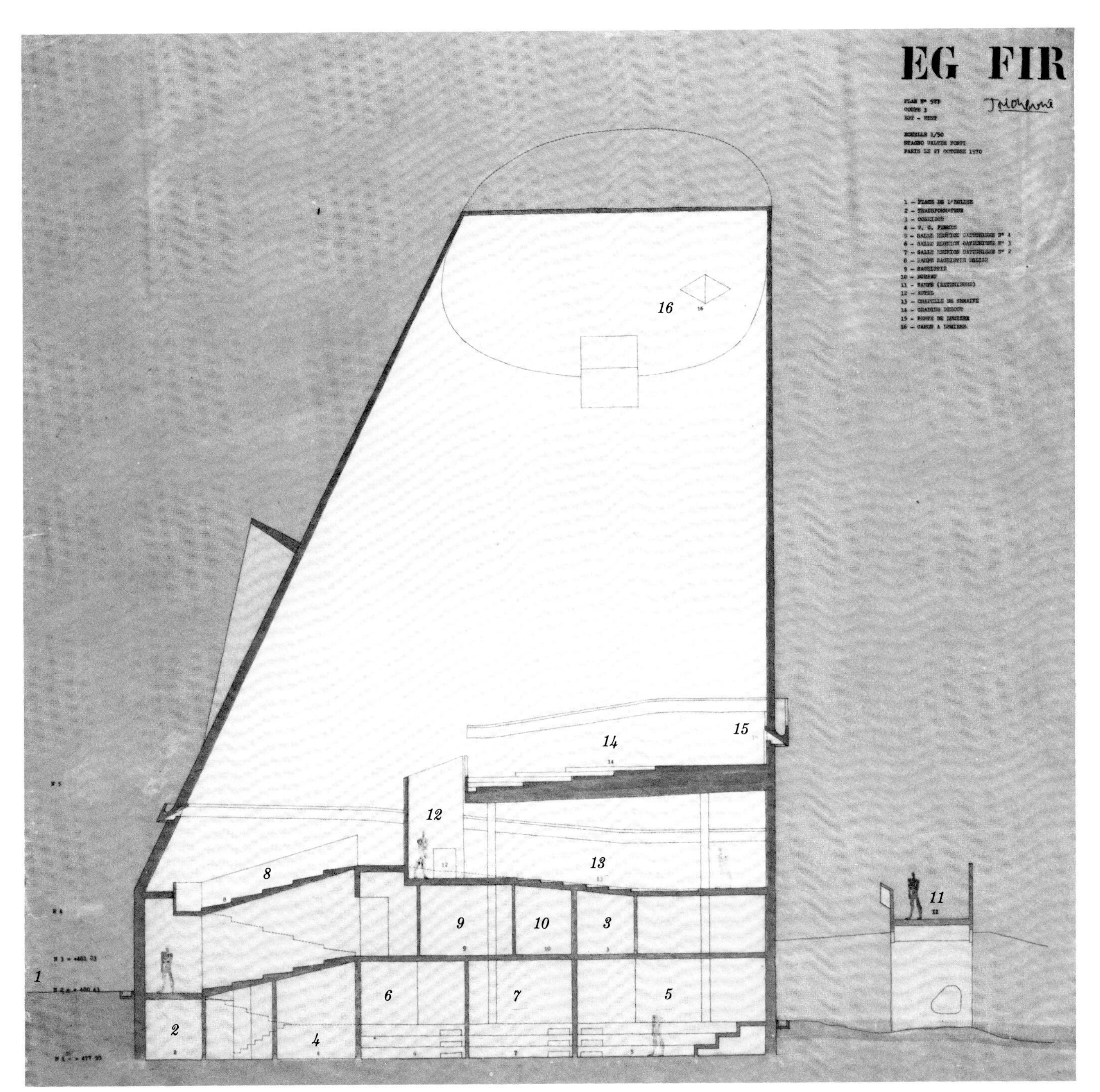

16

1 earth ramp
2 catechism meeting room, no. 4
3 presbytery ramp
4 interior ramp
5 great hall
6 church
7 seats
8 ramp to congregation
9 light slot
10 canon à lumière
11 canal des Baux
12 bell tower

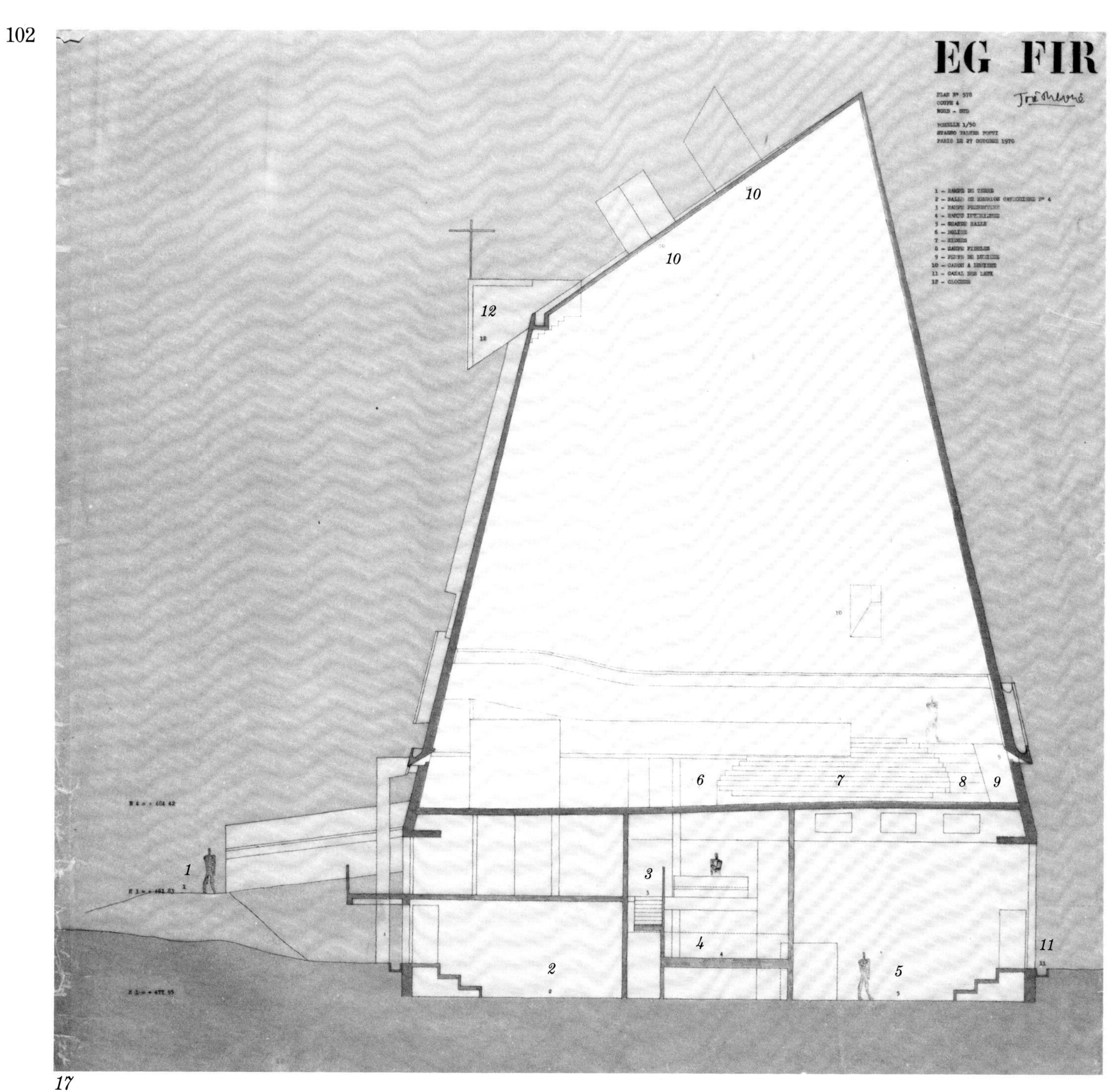

17

17 F.C., October 27, 1970. Atelier Jose Oubrerie, Fonti, Stagno, Wagner. Fourth section, north/south. Ink, collage. 34×33 7/8. (Sec. no. 578.)

18 F.C., October 27, 1970. Atelier Jose Oubrerie, Fonti, Stagno, Wagner. Fifth section, north/south. Ink, collage. 34×33 7/8. (Sec. no. 579.)

1 catechism classroom, no. 1
2 lower interior space
3 ramp
4 corridor
5 meeting and catechism room, no. 2
6 priest's quarters
7 kitchen
8 office
9 recess
10 atrium
11 church
12 weekday chapel
13 standing room
14 light slot

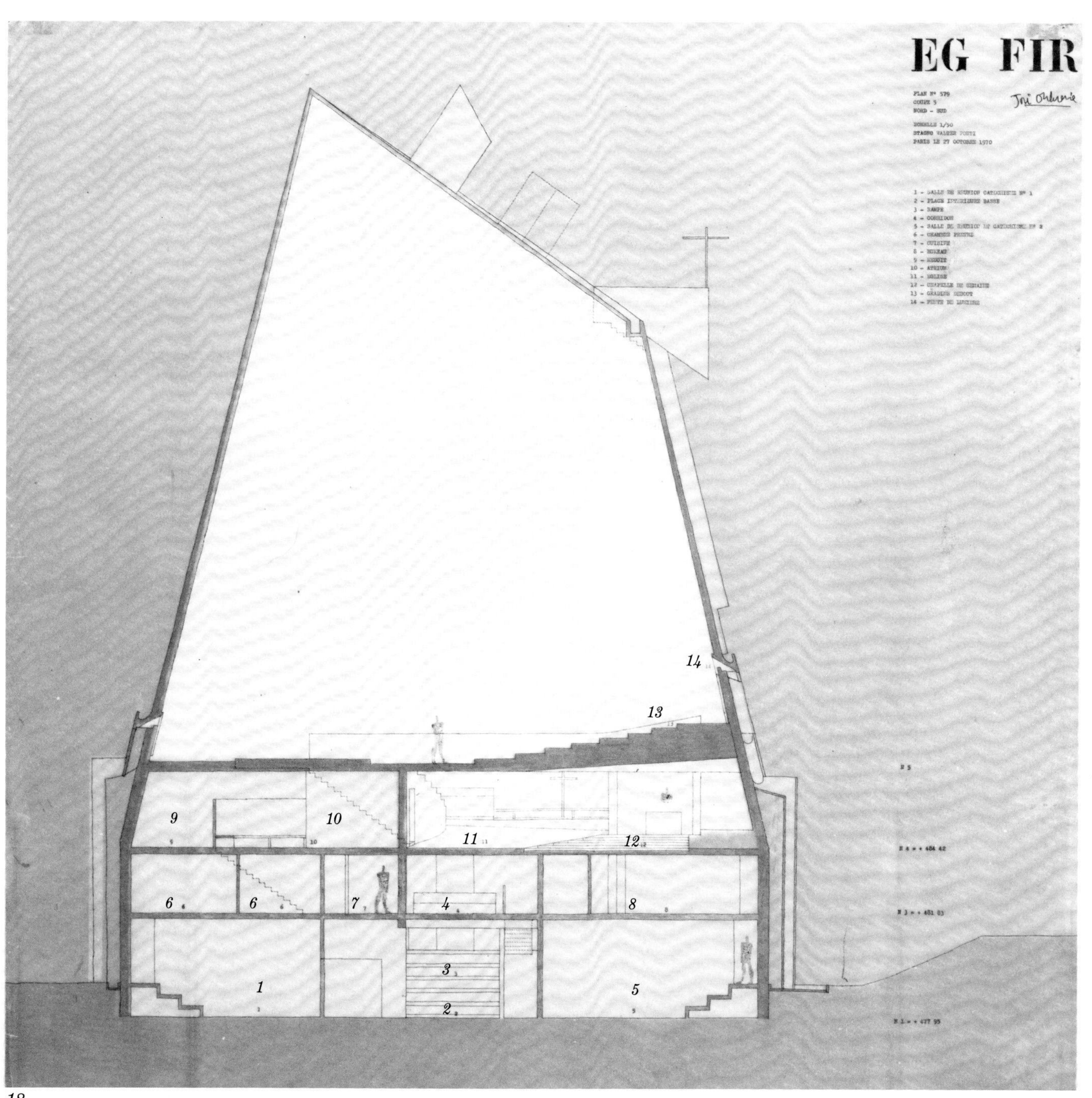

18

1 ramp
2 porch
3 chemin de sous-Marquart

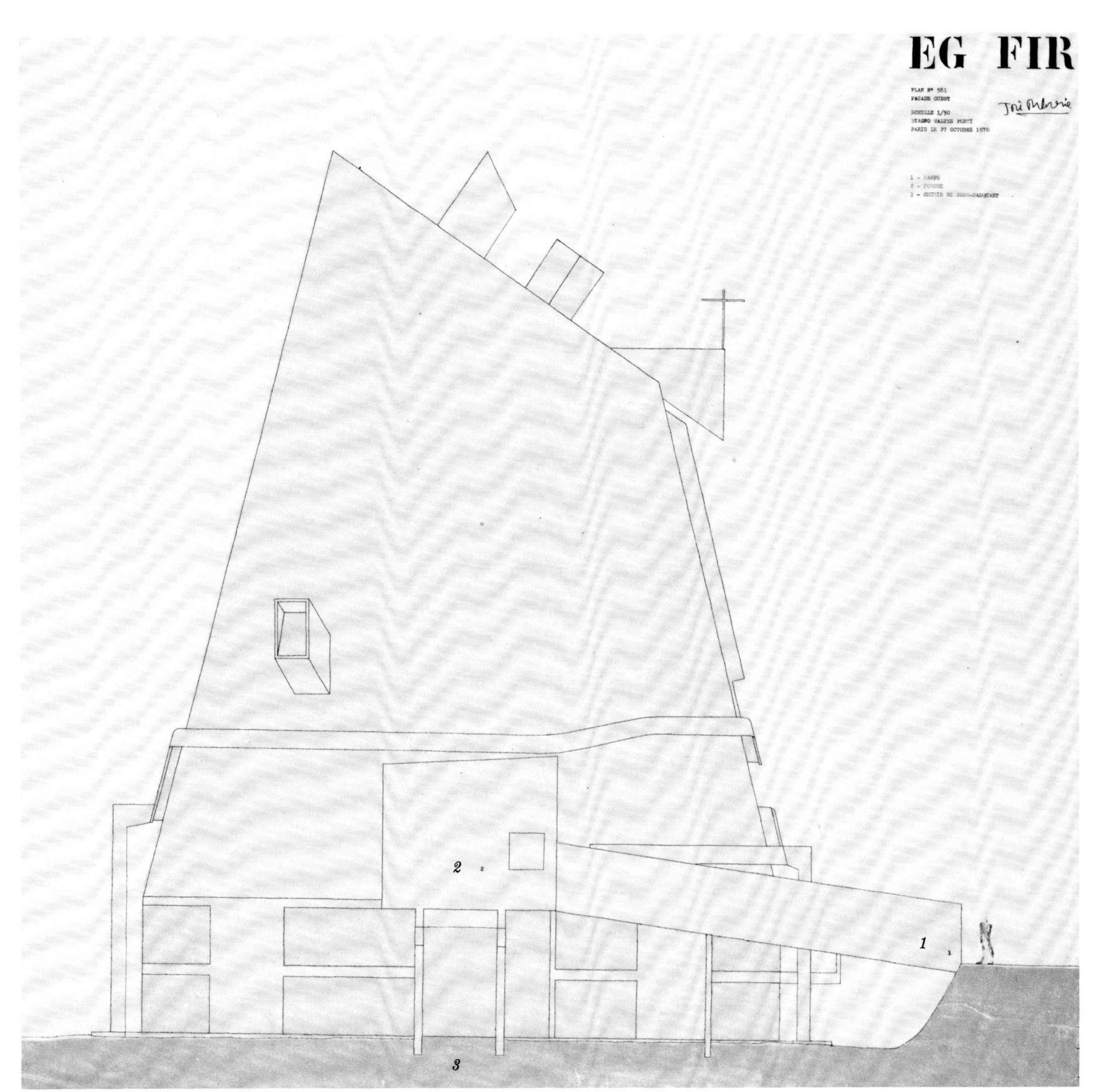

19

19 *F.C., October 27, 1970. Atelier Jose Oubrerie, Fonti, Stagno, Wagner. West elevation. Ink, collage. 34×33 7/8. (Elev. no. 580.)*

20 *F.C., October 27, 1970. Atelier Jose Oubrerie, Fonti, Stagno, Wagner. South elevation. Ink, collage. 34×33 7/8. (Elev. no. 581.)*

1 church square
2 entry, second level
3 ramp
4 porch

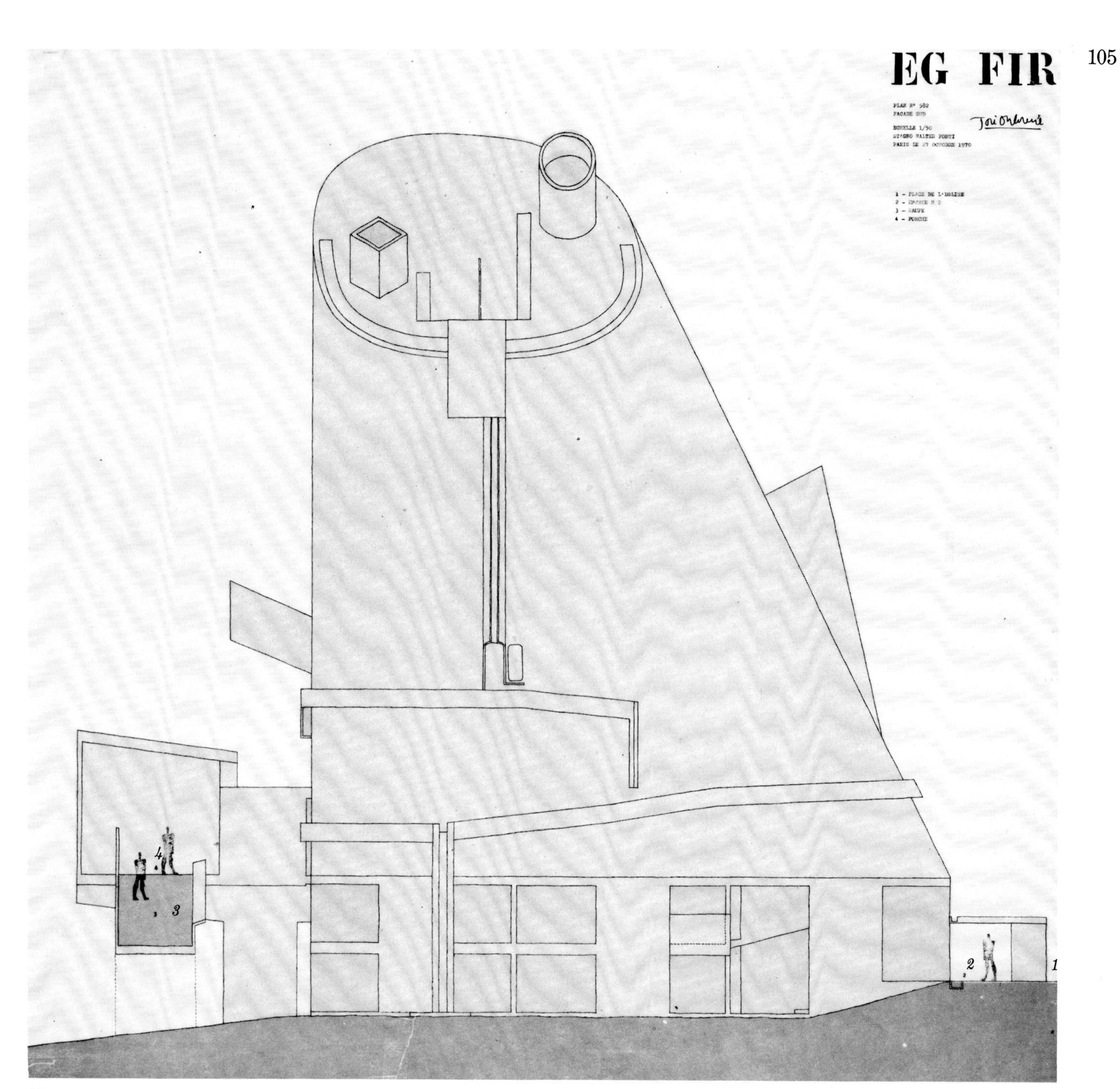

20

1 church square
2 entrance to parochial complex

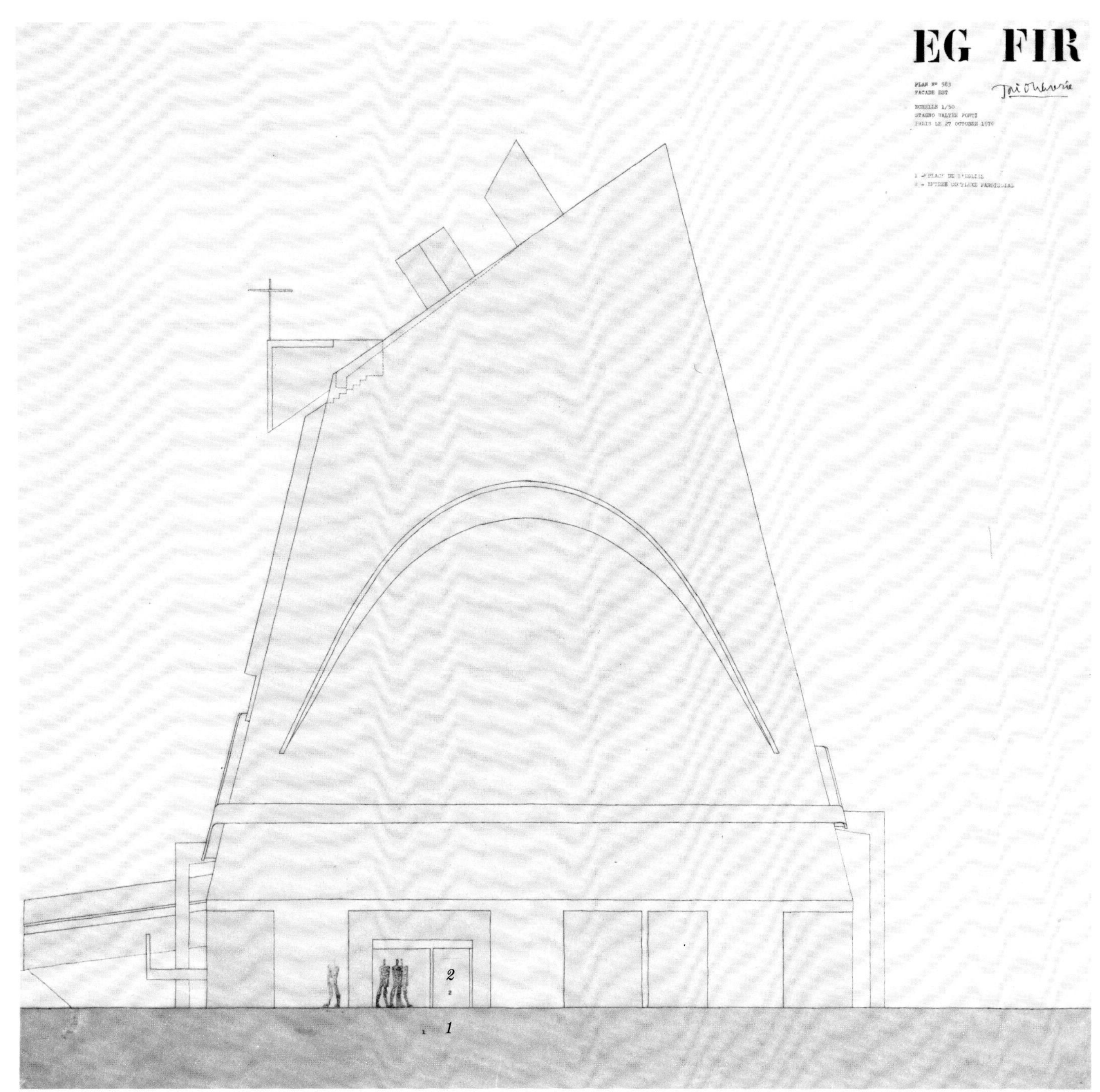

21

21 F.C., October 27, 1970. Atelier Jose Oubrerie, Fonti, Stagno, Wagner. East elevation. Ink, collage. 34 × 33 7/8. (Elev. no. 582.)

22 F.C., October 27, 1970. Atelier Jose Oubrerie, Fonti, Stagno, Wagner. North elevation. Ink, collage. 34 × 33 7/8. (Elev. no. 583.)

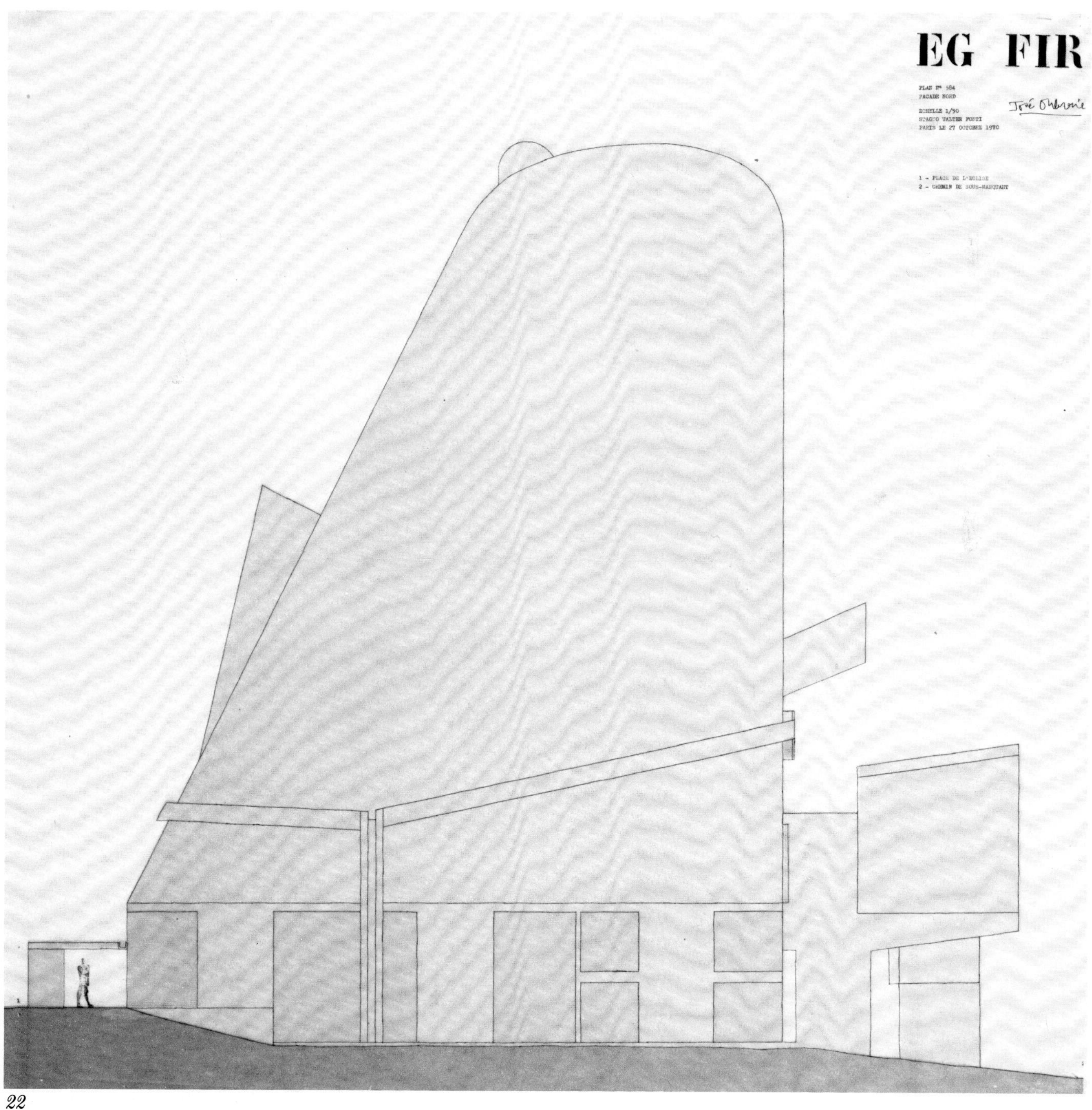

22

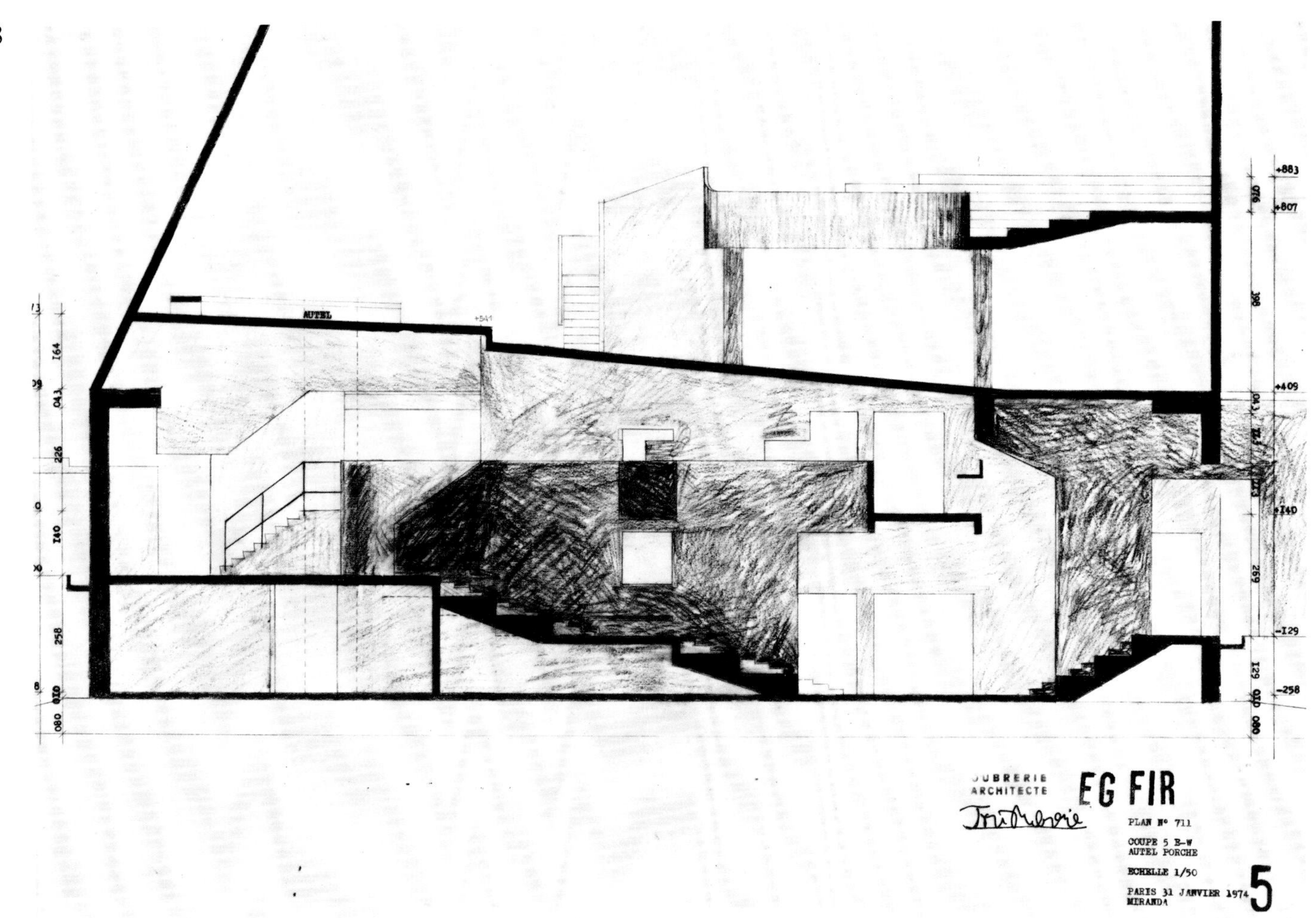
AUTEL
+883
+807
+409
+140
-129
-258
UBRERIE
ARCHITECTE
EG FIR
PLAN N° 711
COUPE 5 E-W
AUTEL PORCHE
ECHELLE 1/50
PARIS 31 JANVIER 1974
MIRANDA
5

23

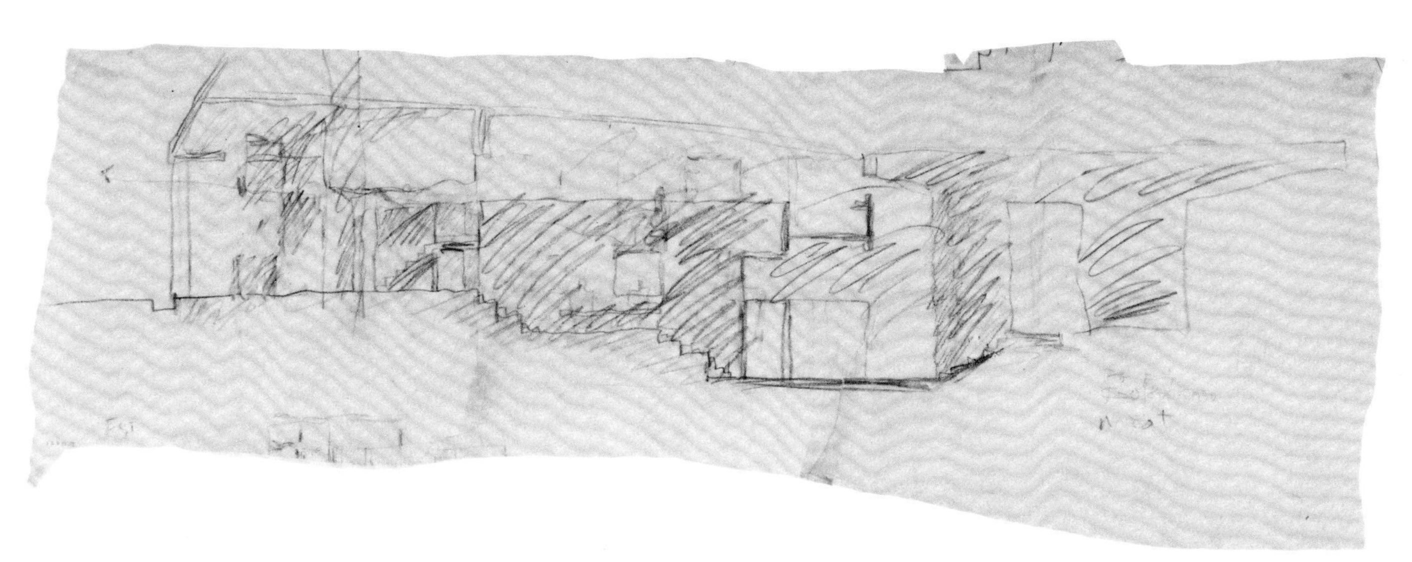

24

23 F.C., December 18, 1970. Atelier Jose Oubrerie. East/west sections; sketch of steps required by fire-marshall in place of ramps. Colored pencil, draft paper.

24 F.C., January 31, 1974. Atelier Jose Oubrerie, Miranda, C. Jullian. Fifth section, east/west. Colored pencil, draft paper. 23 3/8 × 16 3/4. (Sec. no. 711.)

1 concrete exterior access ramp to entrance porch
2 entrance porch to church-open air part
3 main entrance and large enamelled door
4 entry lock and weekday entrance
5 main circulation
6 circulation for weekday chapel
7 stair to tiers
8 lateral circulation
9 seats, weekday chapel
10 sanctuary
11 main altar
12 president's seat
13 priests' bench
14 speaker
15 cross
16 location of baptistry
17 ramp from third level and from second level hall; access for priests from sanctuary
18 congregation tiers, from fourth level to fifth level
19 meeting hall
20 passage
21 prists' stair between third and fourth levels
22 recess and storage

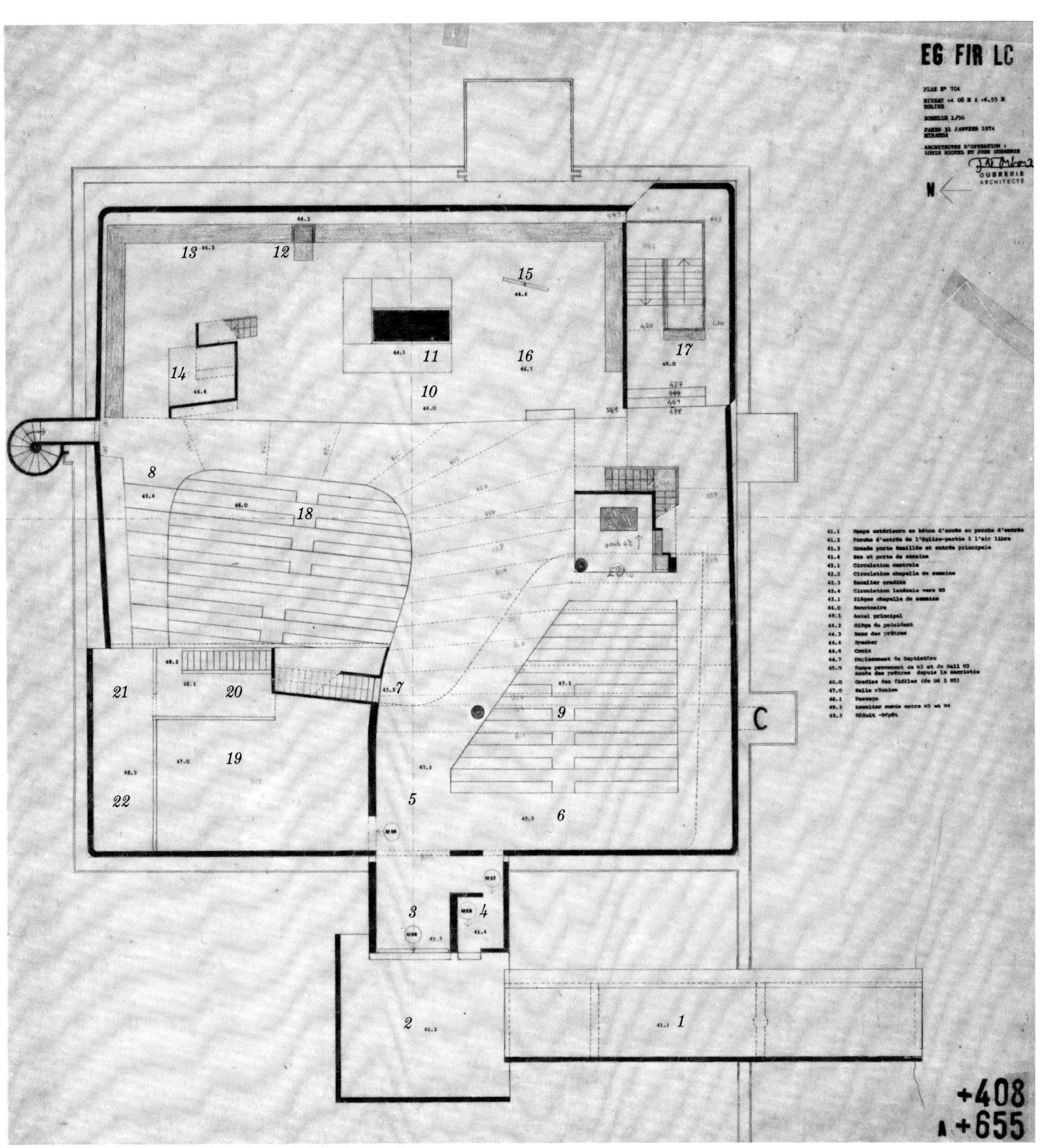

25

25 F.C., January 31, 1974. Atelier Jose Oubrerie, Miranda, C. Jullian. Fourth level plan. Colored pencil, draft paper. 34×33 1/4. (Sec. no. 712.)

26 F.C., January 31, 1974. Atelier Jose Oubrerie, Miranda, C. Jullian. Fifth level plan. Colored pencil, draft paper. 34×33 1/4. (Pl. no. 705.)

1 circulation
2 pews
3 standing room
4 access ladder to bell tower
5 access door to bell tower

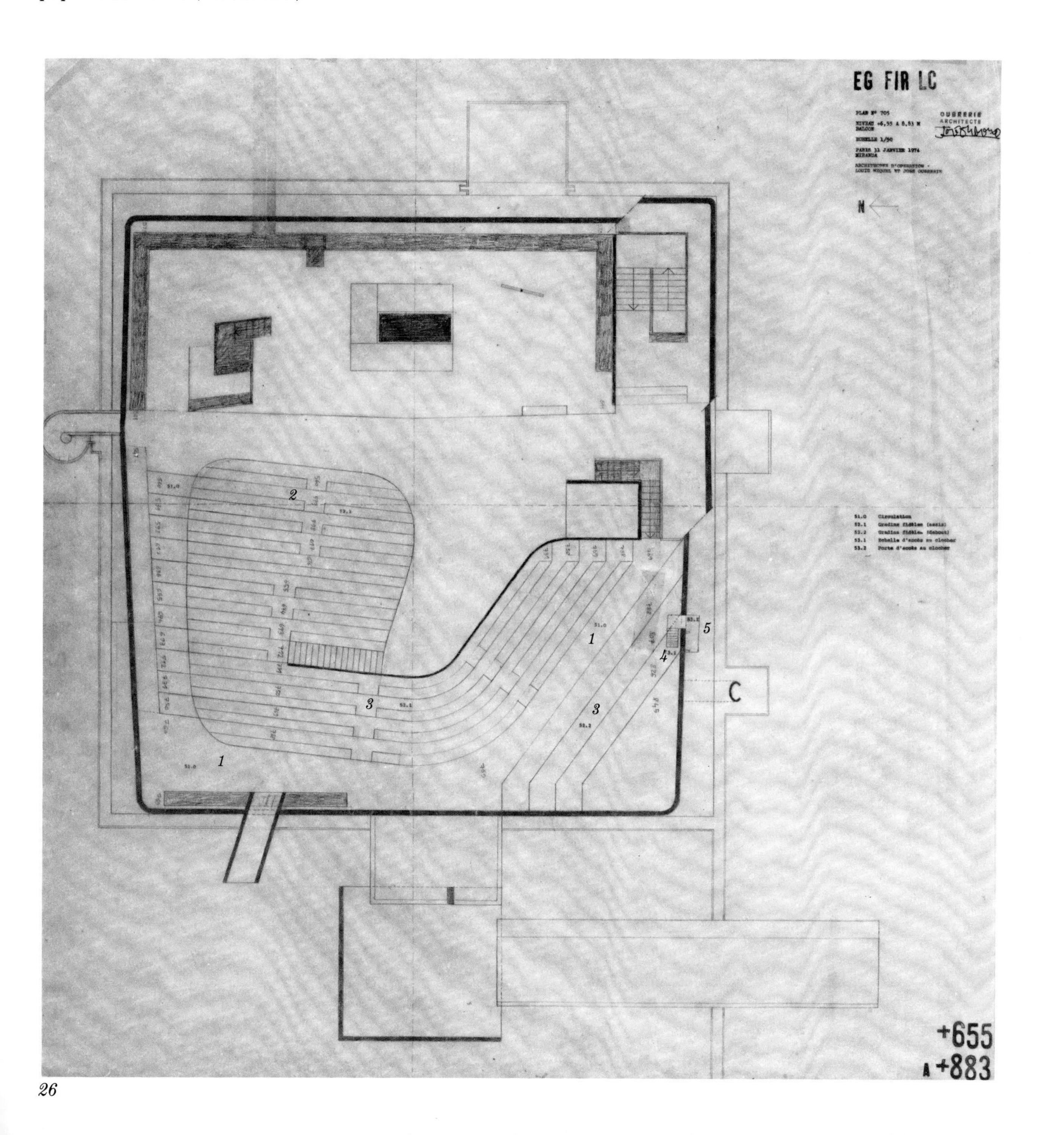

26

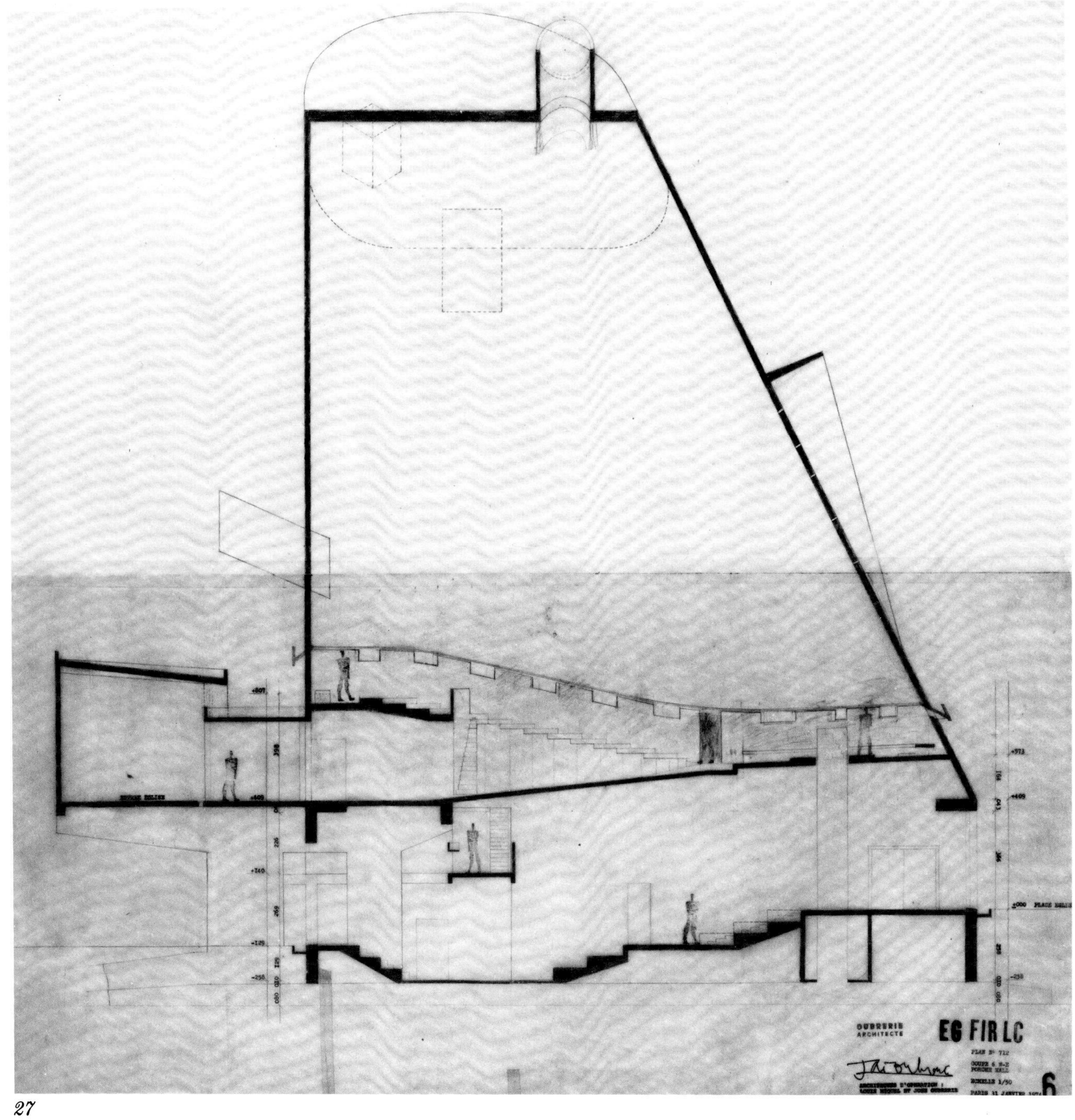
OUBRERIE
ARCHITECTE
EG FIR LC
PLAN N° 712
ECHELLE 1/50
PARIS 11 JANVIER
6

27

27 F.C., January 31, 1974. Atelier Jose Oubrerie, Miranda, C. Jullian. Sixth section, east/west. Colored pencil, draft paper. 32 7/8 × 32 7/16. (Sec. no. 712.)

28 F.C., January 31, 1974. Atelier Jose Oubrerie, Miranda, C. Jullian. Tenth section, north/south. Colored pencil, draft paper. 25 5/8 × 32 7/16. (Sec. no. 715.)

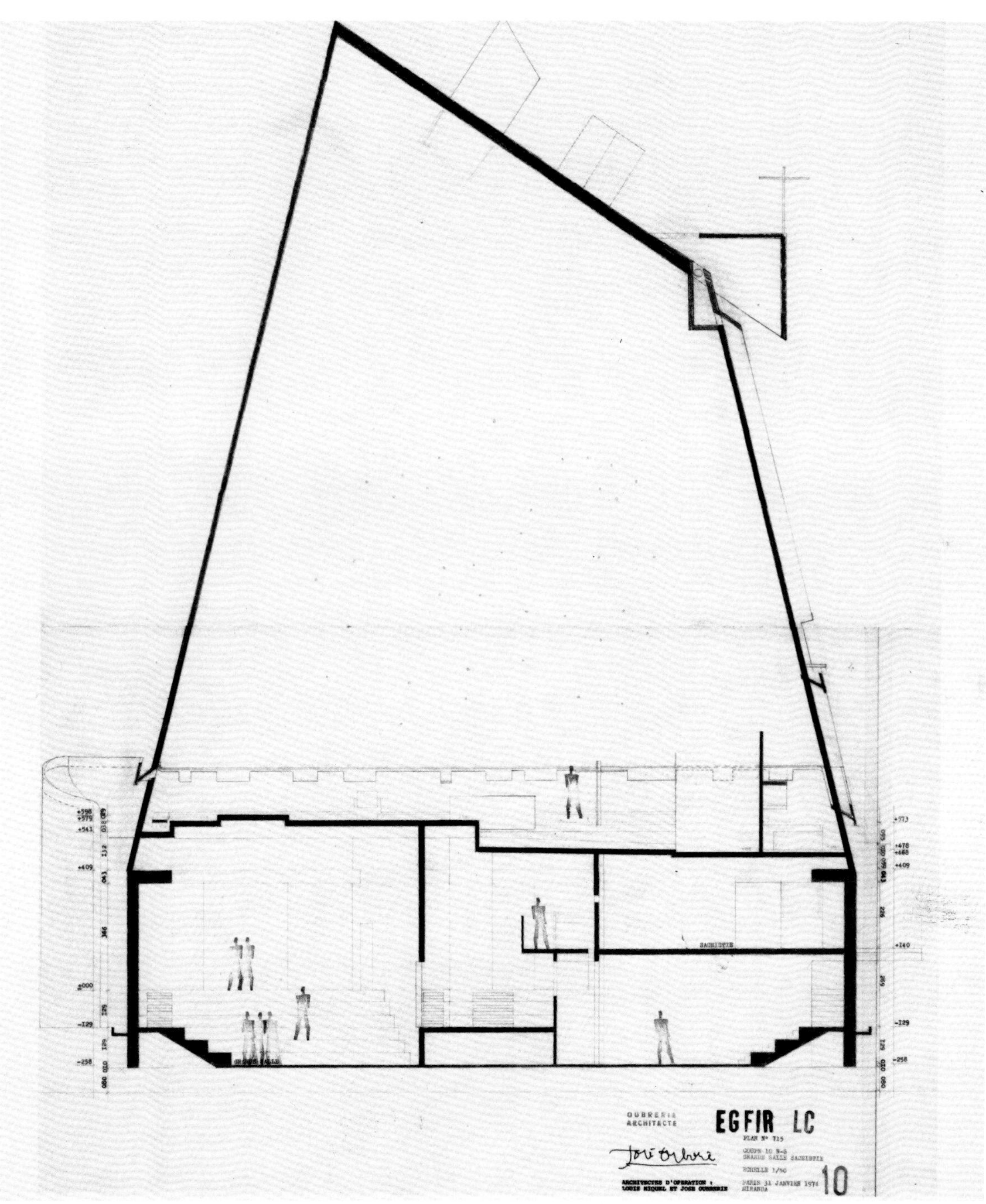

28

29 F.C., July/September, 1979. Atelier Jose Oubrerie, K. Kalycayan, College of Architecture, University of Kentucky, Lexington (Barkley, Cleary, Russell, Sallee, Teriyaphirom). Model. Wood. 49×49×59.

30 F.C., July/September, 1979. Atelier Jose Oubrerie, K. Kalycayan, College of Architecture, University of Kentucky, Lexington. Model, interior. Chapel, fourth level; balcony, fifth level.

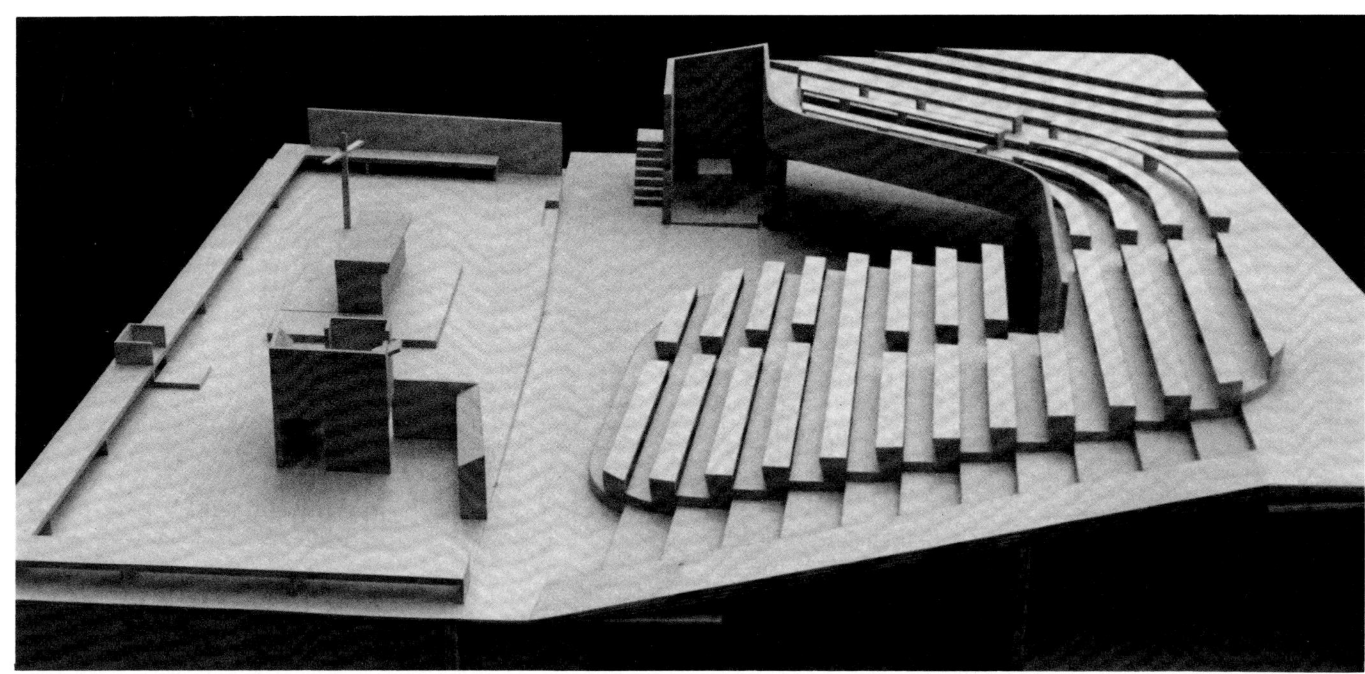

29

30

31 F.C., July/September, 1979. Atelier Jose Oubrerie, K. Kalycayan, College of Architecture, University of Kentucky, Lexington. Model, interior. View of the main altar from the entry.

32 F.C., July/September, 1979. Model, interior. View of the sanctuary from the balcony, fifth level.

31

32

33, 34 F.C., 1976. Construction site; work in progress.

35 F.C., Plaster model.

33

34

35

36 "To become a master:
maître = metre = 1000 milimetres."
Le Corbusier. Ink, stamp. 8 1/4 × 11.

36

119

"ideograms"

april 29
1981 NYC

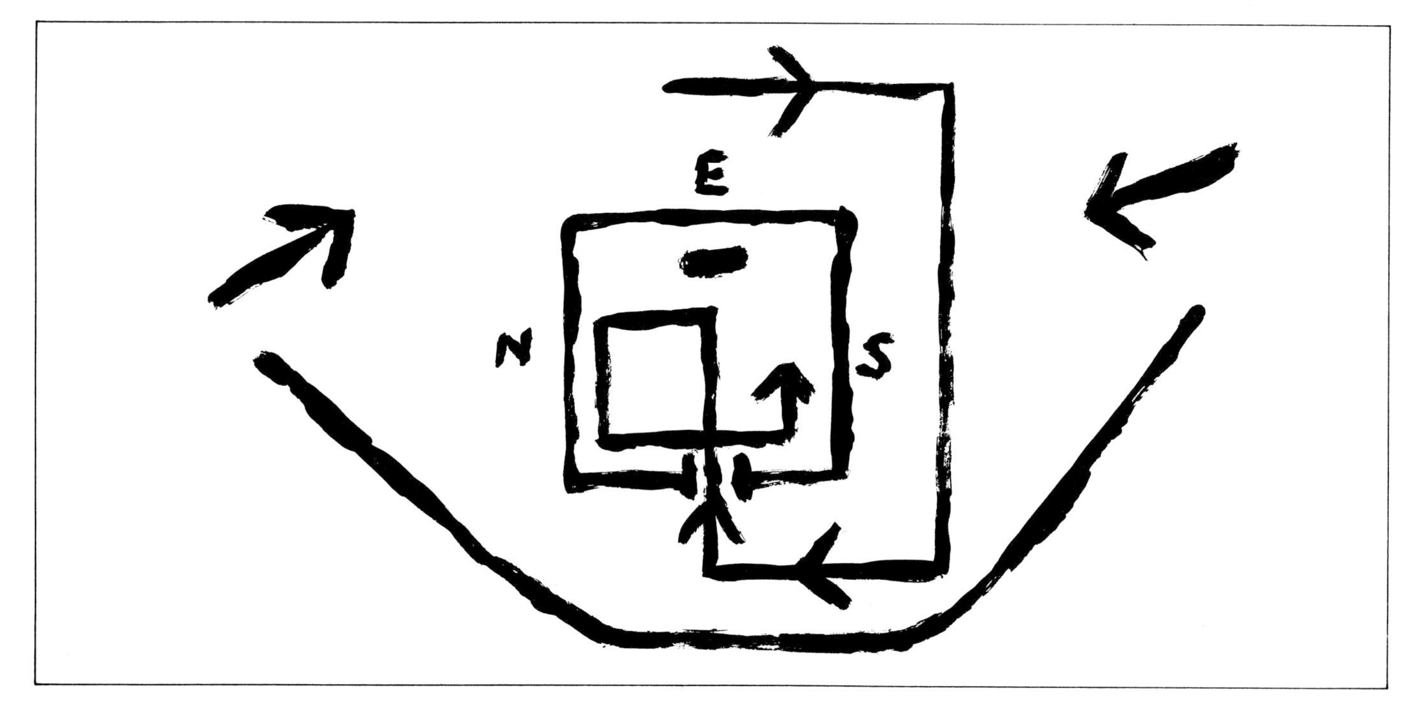

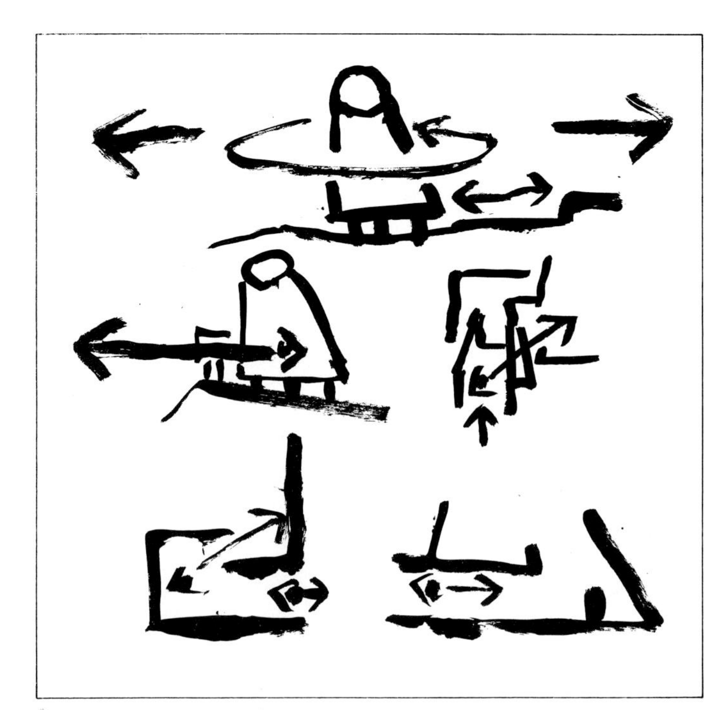

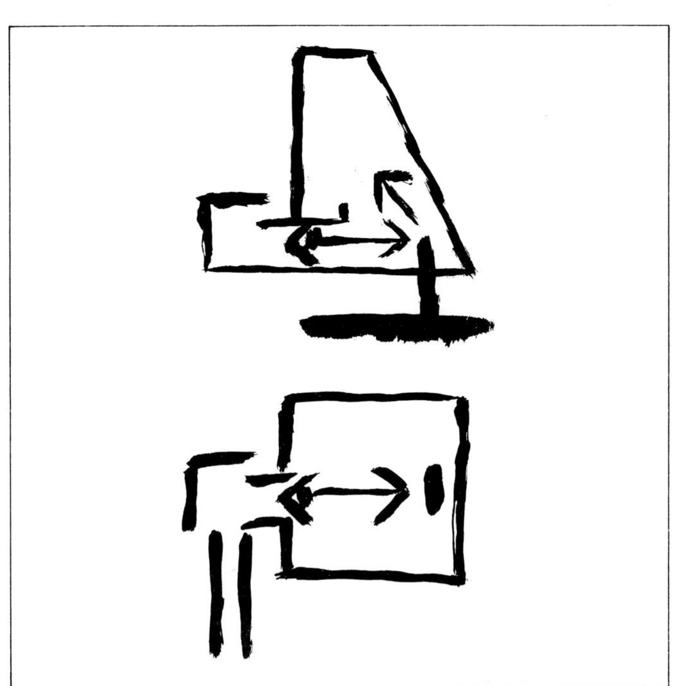

L4
L5

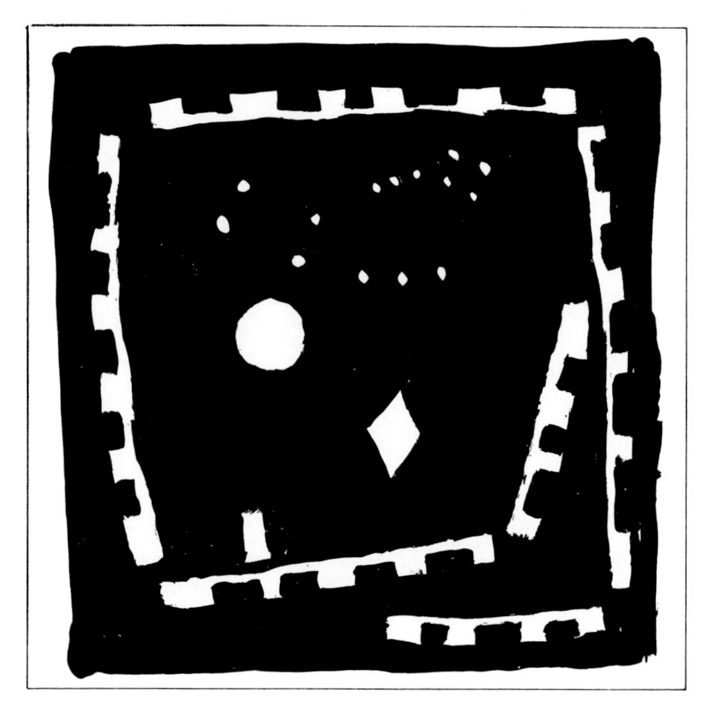

Figure Credits

The realization of Le Corbusier's Firminy Church Project has been made possible through the contributions of the following personnel and institutions: Mr. Claudius-Petit, The Foundation Le Corbusier, Mr. Miquel, Mr. Acceta, Mr. Stribick, President of Enterprise Stribick, Mr. Jammes, President and General Director of Enterprise SAE-SNES, Mr. Pavlopoulos, Mr. Giraudier, Mr. Freeman, Mr. Kalayciyan, Mr. Fonti, Mr. Jullian Carlos, Mr. Miranda, Mr. Stagno, Mr. Wagner.

In addition, the following students at the College of Architecture, University of Kentucky have donated their time and energy: William Barkley, Jean Marie Cecil, Tae Keun Choi, Mark Cleary, Robert Haffermann, Malcolm Morris, Donald E. Russell, Linda H. Sallee, Thavatchai Teriyaphirom.

Acknowledgments
Rene Burri

Eardley Introduction
36 Photograph by Eugène Claudius-Petit
37 Photograph by J. Capellades

Early Drawings
33, 34, 37, 40, 42, 46, 48-51, 53, 54, 57 Photographs by Jose Oubrerie
88 Photograph by Eugène Claudius-Petit
35, 89, 90 Photographs by J. Capellades

Late Drawings
3-5, 29-32 Photographs by Dennis Carpenter
33 Photograph by Eugène Claudius-Petit
35 Ito Josué

IAUS Exhibition Catalogues

Series 1

Catalogue 1
Massimo Scolari: Architecture
Between Memory and Hope
Introduction by Manfredo Tafuri

Catalogue 2
Aldo Rossi in America: 1976 to 1979
Introduction by Peter Eisenman

Catalogue 3
Idea as Model
Introduction by Richard Pommer

Catalogue 4
The Princeton Beaux-Arts:
From Labatut to the Program of Geddes
Introduction by Anthony Vidler

Catalogue 5
Robert Krier: Projects About Urban Space
Introduction by Kenneth Frampton

Catalogue 6
The Architecture of O.M. Ungers
Introduction by Rem Koolhaas

Catalogue 7
Five Houses: Gwathmey/Siegel Architects
Introduction by Kenneth Frampton
Preface by Ulrich Franzen

Catalogue 8
Ivan Leonidov: Russian Constructivist, 1902-1959
Introduction by Gerrit Oorthuys

Catalogue 9
Philip Johnson: Processes
Preface by Craig Owens
Introduction by Giorgio Ciucci

Catalogue 10
A New Wave of Japanese Architecture
Introduction by Kenneth Frampton

IAUS Exhibition Catalogues

Series 2

Catalogue 11
Wallace Harrison: Fifty Years of Architecture
Introduction by Rem Koolhaas

Catalogue 12
John Hejduk: 7 Houses
Introduction by Peter Eisenman

Catalogue 13
Austrian New Wave
Introduction by Friedrich Achleitner
Essay by Rudolf Kohoutek